ANYTHING *but* CHARDONNAY

a guide to the *other* *grapes*

Laura Holmes Haddad

stewart, tabori & chang •• new york

Published in 2008 by Stewart, Tabori & Chang
An imprint of Harry N. Abrams, Inc.

Library of Congress Cataloging-in-Publication Data

Haddad, Laura Holmes.
  Anything but chardonnay : a guide to the other grapes / Laura Holmes
Haddad.
    p. cm.
  Includes index.
  ISBN 978-1-58479-661-9
1. Wine and wine making. I. Title.

TP548.H222 2008
641.2'2--dc22

2007037540

Editor: Christine Gardner
Designer: LeAnna Weller Smith
Production Manager: Tina Cameron

The text of this book was composed in Berthold Akzidenz Grotesk,
Clarendon, Escrita, and Filosophia.

Printed and bound in China
10 9 8 7 6 5 4 3 2 1

HNA ■■ ■■■
harry n. abrams, inc.
a subsidiary of La Martinière Groupe

115 West 18th Street
New York, NY 10011
www.hnabooks.com

To Munir, for everything
To my family, for everything else

ents

Contents

YOU'VE JUST settled in a RESTAURANT or bar for a nice GLASS OF WINE.

You scan the wine list; Chardonnay and Merlot are listed, maybe a Cabernet Sauvignon and a Pinot Grigio thrown in for good measure. Where is the Riesling, the Syrah, the Rioja? Is the wine world really dominated by two grapes and two grapes alone? More wine lovers are realizing that there's more to life than Chardonnay, which has led to the acronym "ABC," or "anything but Chardonnay." With so many wines to choose from, why do we sip away at the mundane? Using the "ABC" principle, your palate will be exposed to wines you never knew existed, never heard of, or never thought you would taste.

"Anything but Chardonnay" refers to more than just taking a break from an old stand-by. It means liberating yourself from the routine, from the familiar, and getting to know different

6

regions, flavors, and aromas. This is one of the most intriguing aspects of wine: the fact that one grape can be grown in myriad countries and develop completely different flavors. The only way to understand those differences is to taste them, to experience them, and (hopefully) enjoy them. And really, isn't that why we drink wine to begin with?

That said, if you do like Chardonnay in all its buttery glory, sip away and don't apologize; there are some beautiful Chardonnays out there. (And Chardonnay can take all the credit for attracting white wine lovers in droves, a phenomenon that began only in the 1980s.) But if fear is the only thing keeping you from trying other wines, take the plunge and start experimenting.

If you're a Chard lover or just looking to expand your wine horizons, this book will give you the lowdown on the other varietals you might not have heard of —or even thought of. Just as with most products, trends appear in the wine world and emphasize one type of wine. That's why some varietals that may be wonderful, interesting wines never appear on the retail shelves or get written up in wine magazines. Some take some more work to find, but all are guaranteed to start a conversation, either with your local wine shop or with dinner party guests.

This book is divided into four major sections: whites, reds, bubbly, and sweet wines. Within each section the grapes (or varietals) are listed alphabetically. The term *varietal* is

7

essentially a fancy name for "grape." Shopping by varietal is an easy way to find your favorites and check out wines you might not be familiar with. (I've included the major varietals from the major wine-producing countries, not the obscure blending grapes you'll never see.) After all, you usually buy wine by the grape name, and almost every wine store or wine section is arranged by varietal. (Several countries label their wine by region rather than varietal—France is a perfect example. Though this practice is slowly changing, I've included the major regions in the varietal profiles so that you can also locate the wine by region when necessary.)

The "where it's from" category indicates the country where the grape is grown. The specific region is also given, although if the varietal is planted throughout the country the specific regions are not listed. Regions are helpful—and sometimes essential—when you're buying European wines, because they are labeled by region rather than varietal.

A list of recommended producers, in alphabetical order, is also included so that you can go to a wine store armed with at least some idea of what to look for or what to ask for. The names represent some of the top producers (read: most expensive) as well as the best value and mid-range producers. Because of the labyrinth of wine distribution laws in the United States, not every wine listed will be available in every state or region. If you shop online you might be able to find most of them, many from the winery itself. Others will appear on restaurant wine lists. Either way, it's worth the time to get to know the names of a few producers you like so that even if the exact wine isn't available, a wine store guy or gal or sommelier can get a sense of what

8

you like. I've skipped vintages because (1) if you're the type of person who memorizes vintages you're not reading this book; and (2) you can drink plenty of good wine without knowing vintages; they don't fluctuate broadly enough to matter unless you're collecting or shelling out serious cash for wine on a regular basis.

The "what you'll pay" category reflects the range of retail prices, although it can vary widely according to which state you live in. Wine prices are notoriously difficult to pin down because of varying state laws. I've given a range to show you what the entry-level up to the most prestigious wine will cost at retail. These aren't restaurant prices, which can also vary greatly. (On average restaurants mark up wines by two or three times the retail price, although that changes according to the type of wine. More on that later.)

Finally, "Dinner Party Trivia" arms you with trivia about the wine or the region that you can spout off to your friends (or a particularly dull table companion) at the next dinner party.

Learning about wine is a journey—an adventure that can be exhilarating if you don't get bogged down by the details (or wine snobs). Be adventurous, take a chance, and try anything but Chardonnay.

Cin cin!
Laura Holmes Haddad

9

WHITES

1

HELLO and GOODBYE

White wine can soothe, delight, or surprise you—not necessarily in that order. It can be fun and lively or intense and moody, sipped in a bar or served at a five-course dinner. Many wine drinkers ignore white wine, relegating it to cocktail parties or summer afternoons by the pool, but this is no afterthought. One sip of a vibrant Riesling, a grassy Sauvignon Blanc, or an intense Muscat and you'll see how varied and intriguing white wines can be.

White wine gets more respect in the wine world than it does from the average wine drinker. Winemakers know that it's harder to make a great white wine than a great red wine, because unlike with red wine, winemakers don't have the skins to work with. It's also more temperature-sensitive than red wine. So when you sip a truly great white wine, know that a lot of work went into that glass.

Many of the white wines in the "ABC" category are referred to as aromatic whites, meaning they are made from grapes that have an intense smell and flavor. They are also unoaked, the logic being that oak barrels mask the aromas of these wines (see page 16 for a look at the role barrels play in the wine world). Ditto for malolactic fermentation (ML for short; see page 16 for more on malolactic fermentation). Some white wines may taste sweet but the acidity in most of them balances out any perceived sweetness, leaving them off-dry; more on that later.

12

While a heavily oaked wine will interfere with the flavors of a dish, these aromatic wines pair wonderfully with food. This is because they are high in acid—because they skip the malolactic fermentation process—and the more acidic the wine, the better it pairs with food. Like a squeeze of lemon, the acidity in wine acts as a flavor zing, nudging the flavors of the food to reveal themselves.

Besides descriptions of the wines, this book will give you a whole new way to look at wine. You'll find that grassy-and-sassy Sauvignon Blanc is food-friendly, while peppery Grüner-Veltliner is the dressed-in-black punk rocker of the white wines. Looking for a food-friendly wine with a lot of character that will impress your mother-in-law? Try a bottle of Viognier. Not only will tasting some new wines be a fun way to pass a Saturday night, you can show off your newly found wine knowledge to your friends or clients when you're handed the wine list.

Before you wave goodbye to the land of Chardonnay, keep in mind that to truly leave it behind you have to let it go. No comparisons are allowed; no "this is kind of like a Chardonnay but not as buttery" and similar utterances. You have to commit to broadening your horizons and jump in full force; otherwise, like after a bad breakup, the hard feelings will linger.

Albariño

where it's from
Spain (Rias Baixas), Portugal

what it tastes like
Crisp, green apples, honey, citrus, peaches, almonds, vanilla, lime

producers to look for
Bodegas Martinez Serantes, Burgans, Ferreiro, Martin Codax, Nora, Pazo de Senoráns, Viontas Rias Baixas (Spain); Cruziero Lima, Quinta de Aveleda, Quinta de Pedro, Rei do Mino (Portugal); Abacela, Havens, Qupé, Tangent (California)

what you'll pay
$11–$25 for Spanish examples; $4–$10 for Vinho Verde

dinner party trivia
Some call Albariño "the wine of the sea," because of the region's proximity to the sea and the wine's compatibility with seafood.

If you long for the smell of the sea and fish is on your dinner plate, reach for a fresh, unoaked Albariño. While it was once just a regional wine from Spain, global demand and better winemaking have led to an Albariño bonanza. The Spanish have been keeping this aromatic white wine to themselves, exporting it only in the past ten years. With floral aromas and a medium-bodied, creamy texture, it's one of the best "other whites."

Pronounced "ahl-bah-REEN-yo," these grapes are grown in the cool, damp Rias Baixas region in northwestern Spain. The Rias Baixas is a designated DO (see page 21 for more on label terms) and there are five subzones within the region. In Portugal the grape is known as Alvarinho and goes into the best of Portugal's light, fresh, slightly fizzy Vinho Verde wines. Vinho Verde should be consumed within a year of production; look for those labeled "garrafeira," which indicates that the wine has been aged a total of one year. These are rarely memorable, but are refreshing on a hot summer's day.

Restaurants have been adding this dry and crisp and oh-so-food-friendly white to their lists in droves. Although the grape is native to Spain, a handful of California winemakers are taking a stab at it, and labeling it without the tilde above the letter "n." They make only tiny amounts, but it's good stuff and worth trying if you see it on a wine list. A few Australian winemakers are also planting it but the wines have yet to make it to the States.

Aside from its inherent sippability, another reason to love this wine is that Spanish Albariño is easy to find in a wine store: The word *Albariño* is usually printed right on the label. (EU regulations require that a bottle can only be labeled "Albariño" if it's made from 100 percent Albariño grapes.) This is a wine to drink young, so don't hide it in the cellar.

Food pairings are a snap with this grape: Think of the sea and the menu will follow. Because it's made in a seaside region, next to the city of Galicia, serve Albariño with any marine creature you can think of: Fried oysters, sardines, steamed mussels, and peeled shrimp are a few ideas to get you started. Adding a flavor kick to seafood such as pesto only improves this lip-smacking wine.

14

COMMON WINE TERMS

Here is a random assortment of wine terms you may see or hear when you hang around wine shops. Learn them and sound like a pro.

APPELLATION: Used to describe where the wine comes from. Certain legal restrictions in each wine-producing country determine the appellation designation.

BALANCE: Refers to the interplay of tannins, alcohol, and acid in a wine. Balance is what winemakers strive for.

BIN NUMBER: Used in Australia to name wines and common on Australian wine labels. This is an unregulated phrase that can mean house style or indicate special, or reserve, wines.

BRIX: A system used by winemakers to measure the amount of sugar in grapes and in wine. Sometimes you'll see the Brix level listed on the label.

CORKED: Used to describe a wine that tastes and smells musty and moldy, caused by a defective cork. Natural cork, as well as wooden barrels, can be infected by the mold 2,4,6-trichloroanisole (TCA), which causes the musty, wet-newspaper aromas. Experts estimate that between 3 and 7 percent of all wines are corked.

DECANT: To pour wine into another container to reduce sediment; also used to let the wine breathe.

FINISH: How long the aroma and flavors of the wine remain in your mouth after you've swallowed it. Also called length.

HOT: Used to describe a wine that is very high in alcohol.

LEGS: Used to describe the wine that drips down the side of the glass. Can indicate the amount of alcohol in the wine; the more legs, the more alcohol.

MUST: What grape juice is called before it becomes wine.

NEW WORLD: The wine regions of North America and the Southern Hemisphere.

OLD WORLD: The wine regions of Europe.

STRUCTURE: Refers to the composition of the wine: mouthfeel, texture, and balance.

TANNIN: A natural compound that occurs in grape skins and tea leaves that cause a puckering sensation in the mouth. Tannins usually fade with time. Tannins are necessary to help a wine age.

TERROIR: This word (pronounced "tahr-wah") is a French term used to describe the climate and soil and everything about where the grapes are grown. It's a difficult term to define and loosely translated means "everything related to the territory," which incorporates the spirit of the place and everything from the angle of the sun, to the composition of the soil, to the weeds growing near the vines—anything that influences the growing of the grapes.

Chardonnay

where it's from
Virtually every winegrowing region in the world, including France (Burgundy, Champagne), Italy (Alto Adige, Friuli, Tuscany), Australia, New Zealand, Spain, South Africa, Argentina, Chile, California, New York, Texas

what it tastes like
Butter; fruit, ranging from apple, melon, and peach to tropical fruit such as pineapple; nuts, such as walnuts; minerals/flint; oak; vanilla; full-bodied

producers to look for
Bernard Morey, Domaine Matrot, Domaine Paul Pernot, Domaine William Fevre, Faiveley, Joseph Drouhin, (France); Alois Lageder, Vie di Romans (Italy); L'Ormarins, Rustenberg (South Africa); Devil's Lair, Leeuwin, Penfolds (Australia); Alpha Domus, Babich, Kumeu River (New Zealand); Catena Alta (Argentina); Casa Lapostolle, Montes (Chile); Marimar Torres (Spain); Beringer, Buena Vista, Cakebread Cellars, Clos du Bois, Edna Valley, Ferrari-Carano, Flowers, Kistler, Morgan Winery, Paul Hobbs, Varner (California); Millbrook, Wölffer (New York)

what you'll pay
$5–$100

dinner party trivia
Chardonnay is consistently the top-selling white wine in the United States.

Poor Chardonnay. What began as a glorious wine from France is now more often a butter bomb with little character served in a plastic cup. It's kind of like the chatty neighbor who you just can't rid of; it's nice, there's nothing inherently wrong with it, but you can't wait to shut the door and get on with the party. There are plenty of Chard lovers who drink it by the gallon, and winemakers love it too. Because this grape is so adaptable, flourishing almost anywhere it's planted, Chardonnay has become *the* white grape in wine regions from Australia to Greece.

Time for wine geek-speak for a brief discussion about what makes those Chardonnays taste so buttery. There are two reasons, and they both happen during the winemaking process. Most Chardonnay undergoes malolactic fermentation, called ML for short. This isn't a mad scientist trick: it occurs naturally during fermentation, when the malic acid is converted into lactic acid and the compound diacetyl is produced, giving the wine a buttery flavor. (Diacetyl is often used in artificially flavored butter products.) This isn't always a bad thing; ML can soften a wine by reducing any excess acidity. Winemakers use ML to emphasize complexity over fruitiness. Red wines almost always undergo malolactic fermentation to reduce the acidity— who wants to drink an acidic red wine—but not all white wines get the treatment. Because certain white varietals are meant to show off their acidity, the winemaker can use certain tricks to prevent ML from occurring. If you've never tried a non-ML Chardonnay, get your hands on one and taste the difference. The lack of "ML" on the label is one clue, but to be sure ask your wine merchant to recommend one.

The second reason some Chardonnays taste so oaky is because of the barrels. Most Chardonnays are aged in oak barrels—usually French or American oak—which gives the wine a toasty vanilla flavor. Not only can wines be aged in oak, they can be also fermented in oak, which adds another layer of vanilla and wood flavors. Just like ML, the barrel can be a blessing or a curse. If the winemaker lets the wine sit in new oak for too long, you might as well be gnawing on a wooden plank, but with judicious use of the right barrel you'll just get a

hint of those toasted wood flavors. In lower-end Chardonnays wood chips are thrown into the tanks to achieve an oaky flavor without the expense of aging in real wood barrels. Some Chardonnays are being labeled "unoaked" to indicate that no oak was used.

But enough science; let's talk about the flavor. The highest-quality Chardonnays are full-bodied, with ripe fruit flavors like apple and peach or tropical fruit. They have low acidity levels, so they're mild and pleasing in your mouth. *Pleasing* is the key word; your average Chardonnay is pleasant and easy. In contrast, Chablis and Meursault from France's Burgundy region are the king and queen of Chardonnay, producing steely and nutty flavored wines that will cost a king's ransom and fill your palate with outrageous flavors and literally take your breath away. These are referred to as "white Burgundies," and these are the Chardonnays to splurge on and that will forever change your views of the wine. (For "bargain" white Burgundies look to the appellation of Montagny, which makes gorgeous Chardonnay for a fraction of the price.) Chardonnay from the Maconnais region can vary widely in quality, but it's also the most affordable: Mâcon, Pouilly-Fuissé, and St-Véran are the names you'll see most often.

Although this is an "ABC" book, it could also be called an "Anything but Oaky Chardonnay" book; in other words, just trying Chardonnay from different regions can expand your wine world and show you what else is out there.

Food-wise, Chardonnay can dominate or act as a happy-go-lucky dinner party guest. Overoaked Chardonnay will overwhelm whatever food is put in front of it, while a well-balanced Chardonnay will complement the food. Chardonnay pairs with a range of foods (except game meat like duck and venison): from crab cakes and onion quiche to grilled pork, braised rabbit, and roasted turkey. Don't serve Chardonnay with your favorite tomato sauce; the acid in the tomatoes will clash with the wine.

17

Chenin Blanc

Chenin Blanc gets around: this jack-of-all-trades grape (pronounced "SHEN-nin blahnk") makes dry, sweet, and sparkling wines and even plays a role in brandy. France's Loire Valley is this varietal's homeland; it was planted in the Anjou region in the ninth century. (Wine geeks have shortened the name to "Chenin.") In the Loire it's made exclusively in the regions of Anjou, Samur, Savennières, and Vouvray in both still and sparkling styles, the tartness of the grape benefiting sparklers in particular. Chenins from Savennières are more mineral-tasting while Vouvray wines are more intensely fruit-driven; Vouvray also makes Chenin-based sparkling and dessert wines (see pages 101 and 118 for more info).

Outside of France, Chenin is the most widely planted grape in South Africa, where it's called Steen. In South America it's called Pinot Blanco and Argentina has been producing a few light wines with the grape. A few regions in the United States have also planted Chenin. A lot of California Chenin Blanc goes into jug wines, but a few wineries are raising the bar and making exceptional examples. Australia and New Zealand winemakers have planted Chenin, although not much makes it to the States.

Depending on whether it's aged in wood or not, Chenin can be fruity and fresh or full-bodied and rich with vanilla and spice. It's also a matter of soil: certain soils produce sweet Chenin while others create the lighter, crisper styles. You might see it blended with Sauvignon Blanc, Chardonnay, or Viognier from New World wine regions. While Chenin Blanc from France ages gracefully for ten years, developing a rich, nutty, yet fruity character, you should drink most Chenin within five years while they're bursting with flavors of melon, green apples, and peaches.

Dry, crisp Chenin Blanc and heavy cream were made for each other. White sauces, Dover sole with butter, seared scallops, creamy lemon chicken, and anything fried (especially tempura) love this wine, as does Asian food, including curries. This is also a great vegetable wine, holding up to Brussels sprouts and any other green veggie. Cheese-wise, Chenin pairs wonderfully with ripe Brie as well as tangy Mascarpone and the strong-flavored Taleggio from Italy.

Lemon Asparagus Fettucine

serves 2 as a main course

Fresh pasta adds a silky texture to this spring dish but in a pinch dried can substitute. If you have Meyer lemons available, try those; they add a wonderful, more intense citrus flavor. People fuss over pairing wine with asparagus, but an Austrian Grüner-Veltliner, a Pinot Gris from France or Oregon, or Chenin Blanc from France or South Africa work beautifully. Try cooking with the wine you're serving; it's a seamless match.

½ bunch medium-sized
   asparagus, bottoms trimmed

2 tablespoons unsalted butter

½ small yellow onion, diced

2 teaspoons salt, or more
   to taste

½ cup dry white wine

1 cup chicken or vegetable stock

2 teaspoons freshly squeezed
   lemon juice

2 tablespoons half-and-half or
   heavy cream

¼ teaspoon freshly ground black
   pepper, or more to taste

½ pound fresh fettucine
   (see Note)

Zest of 1 lemon

2 tablespoons minced fresh
   Italian parsley

4 tablespoons freshly grated
   Parmigiano-Reggiano

1. Blanch the asparagus in a shallow pan of salted, boiling water for 4 minutes. Drain and let cool, then cut into 1-inch pieces.

2. Heat the butter in a large sauté pan over medium heat and add the onion and 1 teaspoon of the salt. Sauté for 5 minutes. Add the wine and cook over high heat for 4 minutes. Turn down the heat to medium, add the stock and lemon juice, and cook for 7 to 10 minutes, or until the sauce is reduced and thickened. Remove from the heat and whisk in the half-and-half, the remaining 1 teaspoon salt, and the pepper.

3. Meanwhile, cook the pasta in a large pot of salted, boiling water according to package directions.

4. Add the asparagus and lemon zest to the sauce and stir to combine.

5. Drain the pasta and transfer it to a large serving bowl. Pour the sauce over the pasta and toss. Add the parsley and cheese and toss again; season with salt and pepper as needed. Serve hot.

note: Most packages of fresh pasta are 9 ounces, which works fine.

19

HOW TO read a WINE LABEL

Wine labels, aside from the various cute animals and graphics that adorn them, tend to intimidate people. With all the numbers and letters, choosing a bottle can feel like calculus class. Here's a primer on how to read a wine label from the major wine-producing countries.

New World wine labels are the easiest to read because the type of wine is spelled out right on the bottle (Pinot Noir, Sauvignon Blanc, and so on). With Old World wines, like those from France and a few other countries, you have to know that particular regions produces certain grapes—Pinot Noir is grown in Burgundy, for example—which for most people is akin to memorizing the Greek alphabet. Old World wines also include the appellation of origin, or place-name, which is an indication of quality. But once you get the basics down, navigating a wine label becomes less work and more fun.

The word *vintage* simply means the year the grapes were harvested. (One exception to this is German Eiswein; the grapes are harvested in January but the bottle will list the previous year as the vintage.) Knowing vintages is key only if you plan to age the wine. Otherwise, unless a year is particularly horrendous, you should be fine. A caveat: Vintages matter more with Port and Champagne, where you'll pay a lot more for certain vintages.

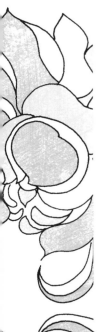

Alcohol levels, bottle volume, country of origin, the phrase "contains sulfites" (with a few exceptions), the government warning, and the name of the producer (with any logo) are listed on *every* label, regardless of where the wine was produced. In the United States, all imported wines list the name of the importer, but you can ignore it (unless you want to find another bottle, in which case you can contact the importer to find out where to buy the wine). Finally, ignore the stickers that list gold medals and other awards; often they're regional and of little consequence in helping you choose a bottle.

20

FRANCE: Don't be scared. Just because you don't speak French doesn't mean you can't find your way around a French wine label. These are the basics: the name of the winery; the classification of the wine (if any); the region; vintage; whether it is estate bottled; and the appellation (AOC, short for Appellation d'Origine Contrôlée).

ITALY: Includes the appellation (DOC, DOCG; short for Denominazione di Origine Controllata and Denominazione di Origine Controllata Garantita), if applicable, vintage, and producer in no particular order. Italian wine labels have a lot of terms to sift through, such as the bottling company and often the color of the wine. Italy created a third level of designation in 1995 called IGT (Indicazione Geografica Tipica), incorporating regions larger than those under the DOC system; this allows winemakers to use international grapes like Cabernet Sauvignon that are prohibited under the DOC system.

SPAIN: Lists the producer, or house, called a *bodega*; region; the appellation (DO, short for Denominación de Origen), if applicable, and vintage. The varietal used is not usually listed; the exception is Albariño, which has "Albariño" on the label. The appellation designation is reserved for those winemakers that have followed strict guidelines regarding varietals and winemaking; unlike France, they don't necessarily correlate with specific regions. There are more than sixty DO's in Spain. DoCa, short for Denominación de Origin Calificada, is the newest, most prestigious classification, but so far only Rioja has achieved that status.

GERMANY: The wine region is listed first, followed by the name of the producer, vintage, and grape variety. (Just ignore the registration numbers, a legal requirement that many producers slap on the front of the label.) The wine level is also listed, which in Germany indicates the sweetness level of a wine. There are two levels, QmP and QbA. QmP, the highest level, has five categories, depending on the sugar levels of the grapes at harvest. The five categories, from least sweet to sweetest, are Kabinett, Spätlese, Auslese, Beerenauslese (BA), and Trockenbeerenauslese (TBA). Eiswein, a sweet dessert wine, is part of the TBA category. QbA indicates that the wine meets the most basic quality level; this is what you should look for on any bottle of German wine that you buy. The word *trocken* means "dry," technically 0.0 to 0.9 percent residual sugar.

UNITED STATES: One of the easiest-to-read labels, it lists the producer, the type of wine and then the region (AVA, short for American Viticultural Area) and vintage. Often the specific vineyard is also listed. If an AVA is listed, the wine must contain 85 percent of the indicated grape varietal.

AUSTRALIA: Generally the producer is listed, followed by the varietal, region, and vintage. As with American wines, wines from Australia must contain 85 percent of the indicated grape varietal.

NEW ZEALAND: Like Australia, wines from New Zealand list the producer and the region, followed by the varietal and the vintage.

SOUTH AFRICA: South African wines include the name of the producer or winery; followed by the vintage, the grape variety, and the appellation (called WO for Wine of Origin), if applicable. About 10 percent of South Africa's wines are classified as WO.

21

SOUTH AMERICA (Chile and Argentina): Generally the name of the house (winery) is on the first line; then the region, such as Mendoza; and the grape varietal and vintage. The same applies to wine from Chile.

PORT: The label on a bottle of Port from Portugal will list the house, the type of Port, and the vintage (if applicable), as well as the year bottled. The word "Port" will always be written as "Porto," the Portuguese word for Port.

BASIC LABEL TERMS

APPELLATION: Used to describe the region where the grapes are grown. Certain legal restrictions in each wine-producing country determine the appellation designation. In some countries a certain percentage of grapes grown outside the appellation are allowed. For example, in the United States a wine can be labeled an appellation (AVA, short for American Viticultural Area) as long as 85 percent of the grapes come from that region. (Avoid wines that simply say "California wine" or "French wine"; it means that poor-quality grapes were used.)

note: According to EU law, Old World wines that don't make the place-name cut must be labeled as "table wine." This phrase does not have the same connotation as it does in the United States, where the term refers to all non-sparkling wines that contain up to 14 percent alcohol.

CRU: Often appears on French wine labels. *Cru* means "growth" in French and is usually used to indicate quality, such as Premier Cru, Grand Cru, and Cru Burgeois.

ESTATE BOTTLED (called *Mis en Bouteille au Chateau* or *Domaine* in French; *Embotellado en*

la Propiedad in Spanish; *Imbottigliato all'Origine* in Italian): Indicates that the grapes used came from vineyards owned or leased by the winery and that the wine was made at the winery. The term usually indicates better-quality wines. Another common term found on French wines is *Mis en Bouteilles au Chateau par,* which means that the wine was bottled at the winery but not necessarily made with grapes grown on the estate; these are generally less expensive.

OLD VINES (*Vignes* in French): No legal definition, and how old vines must be to be considered "old" is hotly debated by winemakers. Some say vines should be in continuous production for at least fifty years to receive the designation, but the timeframe ranges from as little as twenty-five years to over one hundred. What winemakers do agree on, however, is that wine made from old vines is extremely concentrated with intense flavors and ages well.

ORGANIC: The United States defines organic wine as wine made from organically grown grapes and without any added sulfites (see page 64 for more on organic wines).

RESERVE (called *reserva* or *gran reserva* in Spain): In the United States *reserve* is an unregulated subjective term, sometimes used to distinguish a quality wine. Some California wineries use "Private Reserve" for their best wines. In Spain the term has legal definitions about how long the wines have been aged.

UNFILTERED: A wine that has not gone through the filtering process, which is used to remove yeast and bacteria. Some people feel filtering strips out flavors in wine.

22

Falanghina

Tragically, most people know Italian white wine only as Pinot Grigio. Where Pinot Grigio is the ditz—light, fruity, and effortless—you could say Falanghina is the sexier, more grown-up big sister. Pronounced "fal-an-GEEN-ah," it's from the Campania region of Italy, the southern region that includes the city of Naples and the island of Capri. Campania has always been thought of as a wild, unruly region with second-class wine, but the quality of Falanghina started to improve in the 1990s when winemakers made some changes in their winemaking and vineyard practices. The history of Falanghina makes it clear that the grape deserves a little respect: the wines were once served to emperors, and generals in the Roman wars would send troops into battle with a supply.

This is a lively, engaging wine with fruit, herbal, and mineral elements. The wine world finally seems to be sitting up and taking notice; restaurants are starting to add Falanghina to their wine lists and you can find it in many wine shops. (And the more you drink, the easier it is to pronounce!) It might take a little searching but it's worth stopping in a few wine stores to find these invigorating wines.

What makes this wine even more appealing is how easily it pairs with food. Full-bodied, fruity Falanghina has an acidity that makes it a go-to food wine. The Italians know their food and wine pairings, and Falanghina is no exception. This is a wine that moves easily among different flavors, from fried chicken and roasted veal to seared tuna and grilled swordfish, and even works with dueling flavors, like those in an *insalata caprese*, the classic Italian salad of mozzarella, basil, and tomato. It's also superb with another Italian specialty, *spaghetti alle vongole*, spaghetti with white wine and clams.

where it's from
Italy (Campania)

what it tastes like
Bananas, apples, peaches, pears, honeydew, toasted nuts, herbs such as sage and thyme

producers to look for
Cantine del Taburno, Di Meo, Fattoria, Feudi San Gregorio, Mastroberardino, Ocone, Terredora, Terra di Lavoro, Villa Matilde

what you'll pay
$10–$25

dinner party trivia
Falanghina was most likely the grape used to make the ancient wine Falernian. The name comes from the Latin word *falanga*, meaning "the stake that supports the vines," an ancient system of cultivation in which vines were trained on stakes.

23

Garganega

What may look like a lot of g's and a's is actually a native Italian varietal that produces the glorious Soave. Pronounced "gar-GAH-neh-gah," this grape produces a crisp, clean wine that you'll be happy to stash in your fridge.

Soave, pronounced "SWAH-veh," is actually a blend of Garganega and a little bit of Trebbiano di Soave from the Veneto region, and can be still, sparkling, or sweet. (Under Italian wine laws Trebbiano Toscano, Trebbiano di Soave, and Chardonnay may make up to 30 percent of the blend.) There are three classifications for Soave; from the most basic to the most complex they are Soave, Soave Classico, and Soave Classico Superiore. The best dry Soave is labeled Soave Classico Superiore, a more full-bodied, complex Soave that by law must be aged eight months before release. Both Classico and Classico Superiore can be aged, sometimes as long as ten years, developing deep almond aromas; the most basic Soave should be drunk pronto.

Soave has a bad reputation, with much of it a watery mess referred to as "supermarket Soave," mostly due to the push for quantity over quality in the region. But many producers have been working to raise the image of this wine, both in the vineyard and in the winery, and the good ones are rich, complex wines with mineral elements. Winemakers are playing around with variations, making both oaked and unoaked versions as well as blending the grape and making pure Garganega bottlings. Wine geek trivia: Well-respected producer Roberto Anselmi uses proprietary names on his wines instead of the term *Soave* because he's trying to distinguish his wines from the lower-quality stuff labeled "Soave." Recioto di Soave is a dessert wine made in the region (see page 124 for a full explanation of this sweet wine).

Pesto, sautéed shrimp, scallops, and light pastas like linguine with clams and spinach ravioli happily join Soave, but it's just as lovely sipped before dinner.

Gewürztraminer

Most grapes are like a lump of clay, molding their personality to the region where they're grown. But Gewürztraminer is not your average grape. This varietal can be relied on to be floral and spicy in every region in the world. This is the busty broad varietal who's dressed up for the night, a bossy grape that expresses its character no matter where it's grown. *Perfume* and *rosewater* are the first words used to describe this aromatic varietal, pronounced "guh-VURTZ-tra-mee-ner," with *spice* following close behind. The wine world has shortened the name to Gewürz, which conveniently ties into the grape name: the German word *Gewürz* means "spiced." The spice, however, isn't a black-pepper spice; it's a warm spice, like nutmeg or cinnamon.

This varietal loves the cool weather and is almost always associated with France's Alsace region, although it originated in Italy's northern Alto Adige region. Alsace makes crisp, dry Gewürz, while Italy's fresh, floral examples are aromatic and food-friendly. German Gewürz, of which there isn't much, tends to be more lush and full-bodied. There will always be a hint of perceived sweetness in the flavor of these fruity, peachy-pink wines, although sugar levels vary from dry to very sweet late-harvest dessert wines. New World wine regions like California, Washington State, Oregon, Australia, and New Zealand are also making a lot of Gewürz. These are usually lighter-bodied and sweeter than their European counterparts and can be great bargains.

These are wines that are high in sugar but low in acid, so they won't age more than five years.

Because of the low acidity and the spiced character, Gewürz will tame the heat of spicy Indian, Chinese, and especially Thai food, but also matches chile- and cilantro-based Mexican food—and works just as well with meats such as smoked ham and chicken liver pâté. Cheese-wise, it contrasts perfectly with jalapeño-spiked cheese as well as smoked mozzarella.

where it's from
France (Alsace), Italy (Alto Adige), Germany (Pfalz, Baden), Austria, California (Monterey, Mendocino, Russian River, Sonoma), Washington State, Oregon, Australia, New Zealand (Gisborne, Hawke's Bay)

what it tastes like
Floral aromas, flavors of lychee, tropical fruit such as mangoes; roses, rosewater; spices such as cloves, nutmeg, and cinnamon

producers to look for
Domaine Weinbach, Hugel, Schlumberger, Trimbach (France); Hoffstäter, Nussbaumer (Italy); Bernhard, Valckenburg (Germany); Fetzer, Navarro Vineyards, Thomas Fogarty (California); Erath (Oregon); Sineann (Washington State)

what you'll pay
$8–$40

dinner party trivia
This grape is sometimes referred to as Traminer, among other names, so don't be confused if you see only "Traminer" on the label.

Grüner Veltliner

where it's from
Austria

what it tastes like
Grapefruit, vanilla, ginger, lemon, black pepper, peaches, minerals

producers to look for
Erich Berger, Freie Weingärtner, F. X. Pichler, Hirsch, Knoll, Rainer Wess, Schloss Gobelsburg, Walter Glatzer

what you'll pay
$11–$50

dinner party trivia
Grüner means "green" in German, but it's not named for the color of the grape. Gru-V gets its name because it produces fresh wines that are at their best when drunk young.

This is Austria's grape, and it's hitting the U.S. wine scene with a vengeance. Once you learn to pronounce it, it will be your new best friend: "GROO-ner-VELT-leener." (Even the Austrians have shortened it, to "Gru-V.")

The Kamptal region, located along the river Kamp, is renowned for its Gru-V. Austrian winemakers produce both dry and sweet versions and you'll see it pop up on wine-savvy restaurant wine lists, again under the "Other Whites" category, as well as in many wine shops. (Dry Gru-V is usually what makes it to the States.)

There are great values here so pick up a bottle and get in the groove. Although most of it is made to drink immediately, some higher-end Gru-V can age, developing intense, complex mineral flavors.

If there ever was a food-friendly wine it's this in-your-face, peppery, crisp wine from Austria. This fresh and approachable wine will match any dinner but can also be a great apéritif. Versatile Gru-V pairs with virtually any flavor imaginable: from a cold-cut platter, sushi, and every type of vegetable to anything fried, including fried chicken and that classic Austrian dish Wiener schnitzel.

Marsanne

A wine with an oily texture? *Mais non*! This French varietal makes some invigorating whites with a unique texture: they actually coat your mouth with a glycerin texture—and that's a compliment. Pronounced "mar-SAHN," it can smell awful or beautiful, depending on where it's made, so it's often blended to help beautify it. But when Marsanne shines it is truly divine—deep yellow, full-bodied, complex, and wonderful with food.

A "beauty and the beast" varietal, this grape is crucial to wines in the northern Rhône in France, where white wine from the regions of Crozes-Hermitage, Hermitage, and St. Joseph contain mostly Marsanne. Because it is naturally low in acidity, Marsanne is almost always blended, and this is one white that gets better with age. In France they blend it with Roussanne and Grenache Blanc for complexity as well as aroma. (That distinct Marsanne smell can be tamed by the peach and honeysuckle aromas of Roussanne.) California wineries in the Paso Robles region are starting to make some all-Marsanne bottles but you'll have to track them down; you can find quite a few Marsanne-Roussanne blends, though. Australia also has a few Marsanne plantings, and the winemakers Down Under are blending it with Viognier. These intense, full-bodied whites will make you happily trade in your glass of Chardonnay.

Anything from roast chicken and crab cakes to grilled fish will pair with Marsanne (although it's best to skip anything with tomatoes or spicy food; they will overwhelm the wine). A rich onion tart is particularly delicious with Marsanne.

where it's from
France (Rhône), California (Paso Robles), Australia

what it tastes like
Full-bodied, vanilla, almond paste, baked apples, honeysuckle, mangoes

producers to look for
Guigal, Marc Sorrel, Michel Chapoutier (France); Beckmen Vineyards, Cline Cellars, Qupé, Peay Vineyards (California); d'Arenberg, Thomas Mitchell, Torbeck (Australia)

what you'll pay
$9–$100

dinner party trivia
Marsanne is one of the eight approved varietals in the Côte du Rhône appellation.

27

HOW MUCH WINE for HOW MANY GUESTS?

Here is a guide to how much wine to buy for a dinner party and a cocktail party. One 750ml bottle yields about five glasses of wine.

Dinner party: 2 guests per bottle

Cocktail party: 4 guests per bottle for a four-hour party; for an afternoon party plan on 6 guests per bottle. (When guests serve themselves you'll be amazed at how fast the wine goes, but at the same time not every single person will be drinking.) If you really don't want to be caught running out, plan on 1 bottle for every 2 people. (And then you can enjoy any leftover wine yourself!)

If you know your crowd, buy according to taste. But if you're going to drink with un-knowns, plan on more people drinking white than red. Generally it's 60/40 ratio of white to red, but it depends on whether you're serving enchiladas or baked red snapper and if it's a sit-down dinner or an appetizer and wine party.

A few more wine-related entertaining tips:

• Do you have to serve the bottle of wine that you got as a hostess gift? How shall I say this—no. It's a gift, not a demand. If it goes with the meal, then open it up. But if it's something special that you want to savor or it just doesn't fit the party or the menu, smile, say thank you, and stash it in the pantry.

• To slow down the flow of wine at a dinner party make sure there is water on the table so the guests have something to sip on besides vino.

• Remember that it's always better to have too much than too little; nothing kills a party faster than the booze running out. (The same goes for bottled water.)

28

WINE BOTTLE SIZES

HALF-BOTTLE	BOTTLE	MAGNUM	DOUBLE MAGNUM	JEROBOAM
375 ml or one half of the standard bottle size. Also known as a "split"	750 ml of wine, a standard size for still wine	1.5 liters or two standard bottles	3 liters or twice the size of a magnum, equivalent to 4 standard bottles	There are two sizes of Jeroboams: A sparkling wine Jeroboam equals 4 standard bottles or 3 liters; a red wine Jeroboam equals 6 standard bottles or 4.5 liters.

IMPERIAL	METHUSELAH	SALMANAZAR	BALTHAZAR	NEBUCHADNEZZAR
6 liters or 8 standard bottles	Same size as an Imperial but is usually used for sparkling wines	9 liters or 12 standard bottles or one case	12 liters or 16 standard bottles; usually used for sparkling wines	15 liters or 20 standard bottles; usually used for sparkling wines

29

Müller-Thurgau

Sometimes science is a funny thing. Take Müller-Thurgau; the Germans "invented" this varietal, a cross between Riesling and Gutedel grapes. Pronounced "mew-LUHR TOOR-gow," it was originally bred for quantity, not quality, and only in the past ten years has Müller come into its own. These are aromatic, light-bodied white wines with a bit of sweetness and low acidity (think of them as the boring girl at school; she's not particularly interesting but she's there if you need to borrow her notes). It won't always wow you, but it's a nice, simple glass of wine. This is another tongue-twister name; it's usually shortened to Müller, but it's also referred to as "Rivaner" in its native land.

Müller loves the Old World vineyards, flourishing in Germany, Italy, Austria, Switzerland, and Hungary. The only New World region planting Müller is Oregon. The best regions are Mosel in Germany and Alto Adige in Italy; Italy's smokey, herbal, and delicate examples are intriguing. Oregon is making some low-acid, medium-sweet examples in small amounts and that's where the bargains lie: These light, pleasant wines are usually around $10. But as ho-hum as Müller is, it's still a pretty wine that is infinitely more interesting than the dull average white wine served in many restaurants. Because it's so light and unassuming, Müller is also a great starter wine for those who are just beginning to expand their horizons—or starting to drink wine at all. These aren't wines for aging, so drink them within two to three years of buying them.

Just like the grape, think of plain food when matching Müller: Dishes like poached fish, a raw seafood platter, fried seafood, and creamy chicken dishes work well. It's also a nice, light sipping wine before a meal.

Muscadet

Oyster lovers take note: This is the official oyster wine of the world. Muscadet (pronounced "moos-kah-DAY") is a light white wine celebrated in its native France. If you really want to impress the waiter, call it by its proper name, Melon de Bourgogne (pronounced "meh-LOHN-duh-boor-GOHN-yuh"), usually shortened to "Melon."

Grown in France's Loire Valley, this dry white is neutral in flavor with hints of citrus; the best bottles come from the region of Sèvre-et-Maine. The trick with Muscadet is in the label. Most are labeled "sur lie," which means the wine was in contact with the yeast (lees) for several months before bottling. This is necessary because it's naturally a fairly neutral grape, and leaving the juice with the skins and spent yeast cells for at least six months enhances the texture and freshness. While in the past the "sur lie" label may not have meant anything, stricter standards were enacted in 1994 and you can now trust the designation. This is a wine to drink immediately; it doesn't get better with age. French law requires that Muscadet be 12.1 percent alcohol, which makes this an easy summer-afternoon sipper.

For a fresh, dry white wine to accompany a seafood feast, you can't beat Muscadet with a stick. It literally pairs with anything from the sea and is the classic partner to raw oysters. Muscadet is also a great salad wine. Just back off the spice; any lively or spicy flavors will overwhelm the fresh flavors of Muscadet.

where it's from
France (Loire Valley)

what it tastes like
Dry, refreshing, citrus (grapefruit), apricot, pineapple, minerals

producers to look for
Chateau de la Cantrie, Chateau de la Chesnaie, Chateau du Cléray, Herbauges, Louis Métaireau, Marc Ollivier

what you'll pay
$8–$15 (although rare, high-end examples run about $30)

dinner party trivia
The Loire Valley produces more Muscadet than any other wine, over 7 million cases annually.

31

Muscat

Defining Muscat is a bit like herding cats: This chameleon of a white wine varietal can be dry, sweet, still, sparkling, or fortified. To top it off, Muscat, pronounced "moose-CAT," actually refers to a family of clones rather than one specific grape. What do you expect from one of the oldest varietals in existence?

In Italy the famous Moscato d'Asti dessert wine springs from this grape, where it's called Moscato Bianco or Moscato Canelli and is the basis of Asti Spumante. (See page 123 for more on Moscato d'Asti.) A few California wineries are making a dry version of Muscat Canelli, but the majority is dedicated to sweet wine. In Alsace, France, dry Muscat, called Muscat d'Alsace, is a light, musky, floral, grapey wine; dry styles of Muscat are rare, and it's worth trying them. Southern France produces a dessert wine called Beaumes-de-Venise from Muscat, a renowned wine with flavors of rose petals and honey (see page 141 for more on Beaumes-de-Venise). Australia gets kudos for its Muscat-based fortified dessert wines as well as sparkling wines, while Austria produces sweet wines from the grape as well. (See page 123 for more on sweet Muscat.)

Dry Muscat needs lighter food, such as scallops or simple fish dishes, but makes a perfect apéritif wine.

Pinot Blanc

Think of Pinot Blanc as a supporting actor—it rarely sees the spotlight, but the show isn't the same without it. Pinot Blanc doesn't overwhelm or demand the attention but can hold its own, and there's no doubt ex–Chard addicts will fall under its spell.

Pinot Blanc (pronounced "pee-no BLAHNK") is transformed into various styles in the Old and New World wine regions. In France Pinot Blanc is a crisp, light wine (and is also used in French sparkling wine), while in Austria the wine has more nut aromas and flavors (and is called Weissburgunder). German winemakers age their Pinot Blanc to make more full-bodied examples. The Italians call it Pinot Bianco and make a light, herbaceous version that is easy and breezy while California Pinot Blanc tends to be fruitier and is often used to make sparkling wine. Oregon Pinot Blanc is an up-and-coming varietal for the state, and is more European in character, with some subtle pear fruit and mineral elements. Winemakers tend to be judicious with the oak with this varietal because the fruitiness is easily overwhelmed, and some skip barrel contact altogether. It's a Chardonnay lookalike on the vine, and the wine has a few hints of unoaked Chardonnay, so if you're having trouble easing your way out of Chard-land try a Pinot Blanc. Because this wine has yet to garner much attention, values abound, with very pleasant bottles to be found for around $10.

Pinot Blanc works with creamy dishes but goes just as well with grilled fish, especially sardines, shrimp, and even salty meats like prosciutto. The only food to skip? Cheese. Pinot Blanc is no match for cheese, as it tends to disappear into the flavors of the cheese.

where it's from
France (Alsace), Italy (Trentino–Alto Adige, Collio, Friuli-Venezia Giulia), Austria, Germany (Pfalz, Baden), California (Monterey, Mendocino), Oregon

what it tastes like
Pears, hazelnuts, apples, peaches

producers to look for
Albrecht, Domaine Schlumberger, Hugel, Mader (France); Marco Felluga (Italy); Brundlmayer, Josef Schmid, Prieler Seeberg, Wolfgang Unger (Austria); Bonny Doon, Chalone Vineyard, Chateau St Jean, Robert Sinskey, Tangent (California); A to Z Wineworks, Erath, Ponzi Vineyard, St. Innocent, WillaKenzie (Oregon)

what you'll pay
$8–$30

dinner party trivia
Pinot Blanc originated in France's Burgundy region, but lost to Chardonnay when France created the AOC classification system and defined which grapes could be grown in each region.

sesame-crusted salmon

serves 4

¼ cup white sesame seeds

¼ cup black sesame seeds

Two (¾-pound) center-cut salmon pieces, 1 inch thick, skinned

Olive oil

Salt and freshly ground black pepper

For the sauce

1½ tablespoons miso paste (available in Asian markets and some specialty grocery stores)

½ teaspoon soy sauce

⅛ teaspoon sesame oil

The sesame seeds give fresh salmon a nice crunch and an interesting presentation, and the miso sauce adds another flavor dimension. Open a bottle of Pinot Gris or, if you're feeling red, try its cousin, Pinot Noir.

1. Preheat the oven to 400°F.

2. On a plate, combine the sesame seeds. Rub each piece of salmon with oil and sprinkle with salt and pepper. Coat one side of each piece of salmon with sesame seeds.

3. Place the salmon, sesame seed side up, on a baking sheet and bake on the middle rack of the oven for about 8 to 10 minutes for medium-rare; for well-done salmon, cook for about 12 minutes. Cooking time will vary according to how thick your salmon is; the thinner the salmon, the shorter the cooking time.

4. In a small bowl whisk together the miso paste, soy sauce, 1 tablespoon water, and the sesame oil to form a thick sauce. If it's too thick, add a teaspoon of water.

5. Cut each piece of salmon in half and drizzle each piece with a little of the miso sauce.

note: If you want to make cocktail-party salmon bites, cut 1½ pounds salmon fillet into ¾-inch cubes. Cover each cube in sesame seeds and bake on a baking sheet for 5 to 7 minutes at 400°F. Serve with toothpicks.

Pinot Gris

Pinot Gris (gris means "gray" in French) is like the Jackie Onassis of the wine world: regal, elegant, and flattered by almost any light. More of a pale yellow than an actual gray, this dry, crisp white wine is grown around the world.

The Italians call it Pinot Grigio, and France's Alsace region is known for its version, called Tokay d'Alsace. In the States and in New Zealand it's plain ol' Pinot Gris (pronounced "pee-noh GREE"). Austrian Pinot Gris (called Ruländer as well as Grauer Burgunder) is a bit smokey. In Germany Pinot Gris becomes a fairly sweet, medium- to full-bodied wine, but unfortunately not much makes it to the States. Pinot Gris has settled in nicely to its adoptive state of Oregon, where in the 1970s winemakers were the first in the United States to plant this grape.

Pinot Gris offers great bang for the buck, too: You can sip a fantastic wine for $15 and under. Whether it's the light, crisp, lean Italian version, the deep, honeyed Tokay, or a combination of the two from Oregon, it will wow you with flavors of lemon, pear, apple, and a few floral notes. The name will tell you what kind of wine you're buying. Stylistically, Pinot Gris will almost always be a richer, fatter wine showcasing the fruit, while Pinot Grigio is usually a crisp, clean wine with mineral flavors.

Even better with food than on its own, Pinot Gris adapts to an incredible range of flavors, from any type of seafood to pasta tossed with pesto, Tex-Mex, Thai, and Indian food. It's also a wonderful salad wine, balancing the acidity of salad dressing and enhancing the lettuce and vegetable flavors.

where it's from
France (Alsace), Germany, Austria, New Zealand, Italy, California, Oregon, Washington State

what it tastes like
Lemon, pears, apples, peaches, floral notes, hints of spices such as nutmeg and ginger

producers to look for
Alois Lageder, La Colombaia, Castello di Gabbiano, La Tunella Colli (Italy); A to Z Wineworks, Adelsheim, Eyrie Vineyards, King Estate, Oak Knoll, Ponzi, Solena Cellars (Oregon); Leon Beyer, Lucien Albrecht, Trimbach (France); Huia, Spy Valley (New Zealand); Flora Springs, J Vineyards, Renwood, Swanson, Tangent (California); Arbor Crest, Columbia, Hogue (Washington State); Ilmitz Kracher (Austria)

what you'll pay
$6–$20 for Pinot Grigio; $10–$40 for Pinot Gris

dinner party trivia
This grape may be named for the color gray, but on the vine it can appear anywhere from blue-gray to pinkish brown.

35

Riesling

If one word comes to mind when "Riesling" is uttered, it's usually the word *sweet*. But this fruity, floral varietal is so much more than that—aromatic, inviting, and one of the most over-looked white wines on the market.

Riesling (pronounced "REES-ling") is the best-known German varietal (it's been planted there since the 1400s), and Riesling from the Mosel-Saar-Ruwer region is considered some of the best in the world. But wine regions around the world have put their own spin on this white wine: France's Alsace region, which borders Germany, and southern Australia's Clare Valley produce knockout Rieslings, and California, Oregon, Washington State, and even New York are making their fair share. The cool-climate Monterey region in California in particular produces very complex Riesling. (You'll also see a ton of late-harvest wines made from Riesling grapes; if you like intense, sweet dessert wines, drink up. See pages 117 and 122 for more on Riesling-based dessert wines.)

There is a broad range of styles out there, from dry to sweet varieties, but they are all full-bodied, complex, low alcohol wines. And contrary to common belief, they're not all sweet. Alsatian Rieslings are a bit richer than German Rieslings, meaning they're rounder, bigger wines. German Rieslings are labeled according to their sweetness level when the grapes are picked. There are five levels, in ascending order of sweetness: Kabinett, Spätlese, Auslese, Beerenauslese (BA), and Trockenbeerenauslese (TBA). Most people associate German wine with sweet wines but, in fact, about two-thirds of German wines are dry; the word *trocken* means "dry," and regardless of the sweetness label a bottle with "trocken" on the label will be a dry wine. (For more on German wine labels, see page 21.) In Austria, which has its own system for measuring ripeness, the best Riesling comes from the Wachau, Kremstal, and Kamptal regions. Austrian Rieslings, drier and more full-bodied than German Rieslings, also have more mineral elements than those from Alsace. In the New World Australian Rieslings have carved out a niche for themselves, and these dry examples show off the mineral character of the grape as well as some

fruit. Riesling from the States (California, Washington State, Oregon, and New York) tends to be fruitier with a hint of minerals. (Some New World wineries label their Riesling "Johannisburg [or Johannisberg] Riesling," but it's still the same old Riesling.)

The razor-sharp aromas of Riesling lean towards the fruity side, with apple, peach, and apricot and hints of nutmeg and clove and a definite floral characteristic. Rieslings tend to pick up flavoring from the mineral content in the soils they are grown in, so hints of slate make their way into the aroma and flavor of the wines. Rieslings can also have a distinctive gasoline smell as they age, which is inherent in the grape (the Alsatians call it *goût de pétrole*). Not every Riesling has this aroma, so if you're put off by it just try one from a different region. And you can put away a Riesling in your cellar if you're so inclined; they only get better with age—some say decades.

Rieslings are super food-friendly thanks to their acidity, which can cut through heavy sauces and flavors; think fat and salt and go from there. (Some sommeliers think Riesling is *the* food wine, moving through every course with ease.) From fried chicken and smoked meat or fish to spicy Chinese, a glass of Riesling will pair perfectly.

Roasted Peaches with Toasted Almonds and Mascarpone Cream

serves 6

These sweet roasted fruit, with the crunch of nuts, pair wonderfully with Moscato d'Asti or a late-harvest Riesling. You can skip the mascarpone cream and serve vanilla ice cream in a pinch.

2 tablespoons unsalted butter

½ cup dark brown sugar

½ teaspoon vanilla extract

Pinch of salt

4 ripe peaches, cut in half lengthwise and pitted

1 cup mascarpone

1 tablespoon powdered sugar

½ cup toasted, sliced almonds

1. Preheat the oven to 375°F.

2. Melt the butter in a small saucepan and add the brown sugar, vanilla, and salt. Stir to combine. Pour the mixture into a 9 x 13–inch baking dish.

3. Place the peaches, cut side down, in the sugar mixture and bake until tender, about 15 minutes.

4. Meanwhile, make the mascarpone cream: whisk the mascarpone together with the powdered sugar until smooth.

5. Let the peaches cool for 10 minutes, then slip off the skins. Arrange them cut side up on a serving platter. Fill the peaches with the toasted almonds and top with the mascarpone cream. Serve warm or at room temperature.

38

Roussanne

Roussanne (pronounced "roo-SAHN") could be called the Cinderella grape, the stepchild of the Rhône Valley: It's so difficult to grow that the French have all but given up, and when they do grow it they toss it in a blend. Luckily a few California winemakers have started planting this white wine varietal along the coast and allowing it to shine on its own or blending it with Marsanne, rescuing it from obscurity. Australia is starting to throw their Roussanne hat into the ring, and with good reason: Roussanne has aromas of honey, honeysuckle, tropical fruits, and butter, and flavors of lemon and a bit of earthiness. It's a rich, exotic wine that can age beautifully for years.

Pairing Roussanne with food is easy: If it's white or light in color, it's a go. Shellfish (especially oysters and lobster), poultry, grilled salmon, fish chowder—this seductive wine harmonizes with so many flavors. The acidity in the wine will stand up to anything creamy, including coconut milk-based dishes.

where it's from
France, California (Paso Robles), Washington State, Australia, Italy

what it tastes like
Pears, honey, apricots, floral aromas, lemon, earthy

producers to look for
Michel Chapoutier, Domaine Combier (France); Cline Cellars, Eberle, Qupé, Sine Qua Non "Rien Ne Va Plus," Sobon, Tablas Creek, Vinum Cellars, York Mountain (California); McCrea (Washington State)

what you'll pay
$14–$50 (and in the hundreds for some French white blends)

dinner party trivia
This is the only varietal that is grown in both the white and red appellations in both northern and southern Rhône, France.

39

Sauvignon Blanc

where it's from
France (Loire Valley, Bordeaux), Italy (Tres Venezie), Austria, New Zealand (Marlborough), Australia, Chile, South Africa (Stellenbosch, Paarl), California (Napa, Sonoma), Washington State

what it tastes like
Grassy, herbs, vegetal, flint, gooseberries, guavas, mangoes, melon, passionfruit, citrus, peaches

producers to look for
Bailly Reverdy, Chateau de Respide (Graves), De Ladoucette, Didier Dagueneau (Pouilly-Fumé), Domaine Henri Pelle (Sancerre) (France); Collio, Colterenzio (Italy); Drylands, Kim Crawford, Mount Difficulty, Nobilo, Villa Maria (New Zealand); Casa Lapostalle, Veramonte, Vina Santa Rita, Vina Tarapaca (Chile); Mulderbosch Vineyards, Warwick Wine Estate (South Africa); Benziger, Charles Krug, Duckhorn, Ferrari-Carano, Fetzer, Matanzas Creek, Sauvignon Republic (California); Arbor Crest, Château Ste. Michelle (Washington State)

what you'll pay
$7–$30

dinner party trivia
The word *Sauvignon* is from the French word *savage*, which means "wild."

Pronounced "SOH-vin-yon blahnk," and shortened to "Sauv Blanc" by wine geeks, this racy white wine is almost as common as Chardonnay these days. But Sauvignon Blanc wasn't always the white wine darling. New Zealand is to thank for the recent rise of this varietal, often called the "cat pee" wine because of its herbaceous nose and pungent flavors. France has always made outstanding unoaked, smokey Sauv Blanc in the Loire Valley called Sancerre and Pouilly-Fumé after the regions where it's grown, as well as those from Graves in the Bordeaux region, but in the 1990s New Zealand's Marlborough region pointed the spotlight on this varietal. South Africa, Chile, Italy, and the States also have a love affair with this grape.

The tricky thing about Sauv Blanc is that not all Sauv Blancs are created equal. Like most wine, where the grapes were grown is crucial in understanding the flavor. There are three main styles of Sauv Blanc: fruity (with tropical fruit, citrus, peach flavors); herbal (with flavors of fresh-cut grass and vegetal flavors like green beans); and complex (those that have gone through malolactic fermentation or been aged in oak). A grassy New Zealand Sauvignon Blanc is a different animal from a more robust, riper, richer Napa Valley Sauv Blanc, and a more restrained, delicate Sancerre is in a whole separate category. You just have to try different styles and see what you like. (One labeling note: Fumé Blanc is the same thing as Sauvignon Blanc. In the 1970s Robert Mondavi made a French-style Sauvignon Blanc and called it Fumé Blanc, and what began as a marketing gimmick took off and became part of the wine vernacular. *Fumé* means "smoke" in French, a nod to the smokey characteristics of French Sauv Blanc.)

Regardless of the style, Sauv Blanc is yet another great food wine. The classic French pairing of Sauv Blanc and goat cheese stands firm, even if you toss in a few roasted beets. The acid in the wine balances rich cheese sauces (such as cheese fondue), complements onions, and goes with chicken, turkey, and pork as well as any type of seafood. The acidity holds steady for salads and tomatoes, Mexican and Latin American food, as well as with the notoriously difficult asparagus.

Sémillon

One sip of this wine and you know it's not like the others. The texture of Sémillon is what sets it apart from all the rest—a waxy, almost viscous mouthfeel. Sémillon (pronounced "seh-mee-YOHN") has a French pedigree; the French make both dry and sweet wines from it, the most famous of which is the dessert wine Sauternes, in which Sémillon is blended with Sauvignon Blanc (see page 118 for more on Sauternes).

The grape produces wines so soft and rich it's almost always blended with Sauvignon Blanc to give it some acidity, but a few winemakers in both Australia and California are making 100 percent Sémillon wines. Depending on where it's from, dry Sémillon wines are oaked and become very rich, while the unoaked versions remain bright and fresh. In Australia the regions of Hunter Valley, Mudgee, and the Barossa Valley are known for their dry Sémillon, and many Aussie winemakers are blending it with Chardonnay and even with Shiraz. Australia makes primarily two styles: The first is the aged style that tastes of buttered toast and the second is full-bodied with loads of lemony flavors. Sémillon from New Zealand tends to be grassy with less fruit. Washington State makes Sauvignon Blanc–Sémillon blends but mostly puts it to work to produce rich, intense dessert wines.

With its unoaked, sophisticated fruit flavors, Sémillon is a natural partner for cream sauces, poultry—including turkey—and more flavorful seafood preparations such as salmon cakes.

where it's from
France, Australia, California, Washington State

what it tastes like
Mineral, melon, lime, lemon, honey, grassy, nutty

producers to look for
Margam, Rosemount Estate, Torbreck (Australia); Alpha Domus, Babich (New Zealand); Merryvale, Signorello (California); L'Ecole No. 41 (Washington State)

what you'll pay
$6–$40 for dry Sémillon

dinner party trivia
For wines made outside of France Sémillon is usually spelled without the accent.

41

WHAT GLASS, and what TEMPERATURE?

Glasses: Tall, short, fat, thin—there are enough wine glass choices to drive a wine lover crazy. Don't stress if you have cheap-o wine glasses: What matters most is the shape and the color.

The most important thing about a wineglass is that the bowl should be big enough to swirl the wine and allow you to get your nose in there and sniff it, and the lip of the glass should be thin enough that you can get your mouth around it. Giving the wine a chance to show its glory is the reason why you use better glasses, and if you're serving nice wine it deserves nice glasses. (Put nonbelievers to the test: Pour the same wine into three different-shaped glasses and smell and taste them. They'll taste different in each.) And put away the colored wineglasses; if you want to enjoy wine you should be able to see what color it is. Holding the glass by the stem is the custom because holding the bowl with your fingers warms up the wine.

What glass you use and how you hold it make a difference if you're drinking some nice vino, but if you're a $7-a-bottle kind of girl or guy, it's not worth worrying about. The average wineglass from a superstore or Crate & Barrel will do just fine, and even a juice glass will do on certain occasions. If you're one for style, check out the stemless Riedel glasses for everyday wines; they look chic and they're easier to store in the kitchen cabinet because they're half the height of wineglasses.

The one exception? Champagne flutes do make a difference if you're serving bubbly. The long, narrow shape of a Champagne flute traps the bubbles and makes them last longer.

Plastic glasses are fine for outdoor venues, but really, renting glasses for a party is easy and relatively cheap (and you don't have to wash them or worry about breakage).

How much wine to pour depends on the wine. Pour a wineglass about one third full of red wine so you can swirl and sip without spilling, and up to half full for white wines. Pour a Champagne flute about two thirds full and dessert-wine glasses about three quarters full. (And if you're using juice glasses, pour as much as you want.)

Temperature: Temperature affects the flavor of wine. Colder temperatures numb the flavors of wine, while warm temperatures bring out the alcohol, neither of which is the point of enjoying wine. Room temperature is usually recommended, although not for whites, bubbly, and most dessert wines, but let's face it: "Room temp" means very different things depending on where you live.

Ideally you should serve white wine around 55°F, and red wine between 60°F and 65°F. Serve dessert wine around 50°F. Champagne

and other sparkling wines should be 45°F to 49°F before you open the bottle (this temperature ensures that the maximum amount of carbon dioxide is present when the bottle is opened); the warmer the bubbly, the fewer the bubbles. Why bother drinking sparkling wines warm when the whole point is the bubbles?

Chill bubbly and white wine (as well as rosé) in the fridge for at least two hours before the guests arrive. The fastest way to chill a bottle is to fill an ice bucket or whatever vessel you have halfway with water and the remaining half with ice, along with about ¼ cup of salt, and submerge the bottle—in fifteen minutes you'll have a nice chilled bottle, ready to drink (the salt lowers the freezing point of the water).

Don't put a bottle of wine in the freezer—not only will you forget about it, causing a minor explosion, but major swings in temperature will ruin the flavors of a wine.

Decanting: If your closet is full of crystal decanters (a long-forgotten wedding gift) and you don't know what to do with them, here's your answer. Wine is decanted to let it breathe (the same thing that happens when you swirl it in a glass) and to get rid of the sediment, which is only an issue with older wines. (The sediment doesn't look so nice floating in your glass, and it can also taste bitter.) Sometimes decanting a red wine such as Cabernet Sauvignon, Zinfandel, or Barolo can mellow out the tannins, but usually a restaurant will only pull out the decanter for an older bottle. White wines and dessert wines are almost never decanted, with the exception of vintage Port. You don't need to decant the average wine, but it can be a fancy move to try at a dinner party. If you do decant, pour the wine into the decanter at least ten minutes before you plan to drink it and up to four hours for really big red wines like Barbarescos.

43

Vermentino

where it's from
France (Rhône, Corsica), Italy (Liguria, Tuscany, Sardinia), California (Paso Robles)

what it tastes like
Crisp, citrus, herbal, green apples

producers to look for
Domaine de Fontlade, Domaine de Saint-Ser (France); Antinori, "Canayli" Argiolas Costamolino, Cantina del Vermentino, Pala, Sella & Mosca, Gallura Yves Leccia (Italy); Tablas Creek, Uvaggio (California)

what you'll pay
$9–$20

dinner party trivia
In the Rhône, Vermentino is known as Rolle.

If your vacation days are a distant memory and you need an escape in a bottle, pour yourself a glass of Vermentino (pronounced "vehr-men-TEEN-oh") and dream of the Italian Riviera. An Italian varietal, it's grown in the Gallura region in Sardinia as well as Liguria and Tuscany and in France (on the island of Corsica), where it's both blended and bottled on its own.

Although these are crisp, dry whites, you'll see regional differences. Vermentino from Sardinia is less acidic and a bit rounder and riper than the Ligurian version. (Vermentino di Gallura is Sardinia's only appellation with DOCG status; see page 21 for more on labeling.) California has been planting more of this grape, producing medium-bodied wines with citrus, pear, and mineral flavors. These are everyday wines, not meant for the cellar. (Wine geek note: Vermentino is thought to be the same grape as Malvasia.)

And they're light on the wallet, too; you can find a good bottle for $12 to $18. This sassy white can start as cocktails and stay for dinner. Vermentino eases right into the main course, especially with calamari, grilled shrimp, pasta with tuna and capers, or chicken; bold flavors such as garlicky aioli and pesto; and light dishes such as green bean salad and stir-fried veggies.

Viognier

Lush, full-bodied Viognier has been touted as "the next Chardonnay," but so far wine drinkers haven't come on board the way winemakers would hope. It's hard to understand why. Is it the name? (It's pronounced "VEE-ohn-yay.") Is it the flavor, which is fruit- and spice-driven? There is absolutely no reason not to love this wine.

The French certainly do: It defines the Condrieu district in the northern Rhône Valley, where it's worshipped as a rich, complex wine. California winemakers are planting Viognier with a passion in regions from Mendocino to Santa Barbara and everywhere in between and producing styles that are just as varied: Some age in oak and some in stainless steel, which makes for very different wines. Because it contains compounds that are also present in Riesling and Muscat grapes, the nose is very floral. These delicate notes are easily overwhelmed by oak, so some New World Viognier ends up tasting just like overoaked Chardonnay.

Viognier from the southern French region of Languedoc-Roussillon is the place to look for bargains; it is less intense than Viognier from the Rhône and California but maintains bright fruit and honeysuckle flavors and is fabulous with food—for a lot less money. The state of Virginia, with its long, warm summers, has been very successful with Viognier and produces some rich, full-bodied examples. Australia's Viognier has a lot of fruit and a soft texture. Viognier is readily available in restaurants and wine shops, usually under the category "Other Whites."

Viognier needs a meal to match it. Where it would overwhelm grilled fish, Viognier explodes with dishes like seared scallops or butternut squash soup. The fruit characteristics of Viognier pop when served with fruit-based dishes, such as pork with sautéed apples or roasted peaches, chicken braised with raisins, sweet vegetables like sweet potatoes and butternut squash, and rich seafood like lobster. Even Latin American cuisine and fusion dishes such as mango and chile prawns pair perfectly with the bold flavors of Viognier. And a sommelier friend raves about Condrieu alongside truffled risotto.

where it's from
France (Rhône, Languedoc-Roussillon), Australia (Eden Valley, McClaren Vale), California, Virginia

what it tastes like
Peaches, apricots, honeysuckle; some spice, such as nutmeg

producers to look for
Domaine de Gourgazaud, E. Guigal, Georges Vernay (Condrieu), Robert Niero, Yves Guilleron (Languedoc-Roussillon); Kangarilla, Oxford Landing, Yalumba (Australia); Alban Vineyards, Calera, Eberle, Garretson Wine Company, Graff Family Vineyards, Kunde Estates, Peay Vineyards, Qupé, Robert Hall, Tablas Creek (California); Chrysalis Vineyards, Horton Vineyards, King Family Vineyards (Virginia)

what you'll pay
$10–$200 for Viognier from Condrieu; $10–$60 for Viognier from other regions

dinner party trivia
Viognier took off in California in the 1990s and now more than thirty wineries produce Viognier in regions throughout the state, producing four times the amount of Viognier that comes from France.

45

reds

A WHOLE
new WORLD

Now that the ABC rule has been established, it's time to look at red wines.

The rule could just as easily be applied to red wine in the form of Anything But Cabernet Sauvignon, or "ABM," Anything But Merlot. If Chardonnay dominates the white wine side of the wine list, then Cabernet and Merlot easily take over the red list while inspiring, interesting reds like Grenache, Nebbiolo, Petite Sirah, and Malbec are left to fend for themselves. White wine drinkers seem to fear the bold, aggressive tannins of red wine or recoil at what some friends of mine have called "stinkiness," the earthy, mushroomy aromas that accompany many reds. White wine is just…easier, they say. Maybe that's why they embrace the easy, friendly, fruit-forward red wines that dominate so many wine lists—they're easy choices, with nothing that stands out or offends.

It's time to change that. There are so many—so many—interesting red wines out there that there's no reason not to find one that suits you. Red wines can be bold, soft, fruity, smooth, or aggressive and powerful. Whatever you're feeling—angry, mellow, tired, or ready to party—there's a red wine to match your mood. And while plenty of reds are great for sipping, most reds take on a whole new life when served with a meal. Spicy Syrah fires up a winter night (and a bowl of lamb stew); bold, fruity Zinfandel will be the star of the backyard barbeque, matching up to those platters of grilled meat; elegant Pinot Noir will make you want to curl up on your sofa with a bottle and call it a night; and a light, fruity Beaujolais will have you sipping red wine all summer long. That's not to say that there aren't life-changing Cabernets out there, or rich, velvety Merlots that will make your legs buckle. But as they do with Chardonnay, so many wine drinkers simply reach for the easiest wine instead of taking a chance on something that most often will be ten times more interesting than that mediocre Cabernet or Merlot. You'll only learn what you like (and dislike) by tasting, so grab that bottle off the shelf (or listen to the wine guy or gal when they recommend something) and give it a go. Just because you don't like one particular bottle of red wine doesn't mean the whole deal is off. There are so many wine regions, varietals, and winemakers out there that it's silly not to take advantage of them and discover what you like.

In addition to the single varietals, red blends will have you begging for more; blending red grapes is one of the backbones of winemaking, taking a little of this to balance a little of that. Depending on where they're from, there are great values and the perfect weeknight bottle. Besides enhancing your meal, there is evidence from hundreds of researchers and health studies that a glass of red wine a night can benefit your health (apparently, the compound resveratrol that is naturally present in grape skins is to thank for this). So give that white wine (or Cab or Merlot) the night off and dip into something more thought-provoking.

Barbera

where it's from
Italy (Piedmont), California
(El Dorado, Central Valley,
Paso Robles, Sonoma)

what it tastes like
Chocolate, blackberries, figs,
licorice, cherries, black cherries

producers to look for
Cascina Val de Prete, Mascarello,
Renato Ratti (Barbera d'Alba),
Braida, Giacomo Bologna, Vietti
(Barbera d'Asti) (Italy); Boeger,
Imagery, Kunde, Monte Volpe
Enotria, Preston, Renwood,
Sebastiani, Seghesio, Wild Horse
(California)

what you'll pay
$10–$40

dinner party trivia
Barbera is the most widely
planted grape in Piedmont.

If you order a carafe of wine in a restaurant in Piedmont, Italy, chances are it will be Barbera. Pronounced "bar-BARE-ah," it made a comeback in the 1980s after being dismissed as a simplistic red wine. For years Barbera was an afterthought in the region known for Nebbiolo, getting the second-best vineyard sites and the second-best barrels. But Barbera is back, producing full-bodied, berry- and chocolate-flavored wines without too many pesky tannins. Some Italian winemakers use oak and some skip it completely, a topic that is highly controversial among Piemontese winemakers. Under Italian wine law up to 10 percent of another varietal, usually Nebbiolo, is allowed in Barbera, which gives the wines structure and depth.

There are five DOC regions in Piedmont that grow Barbera, but the best are from the towns of Asti and Alba (and labeled Barbera d'Asti and Barbera d'Alba). Barbera d'Alba is a bit bigger and more full-flavored than those from Asti—and a bit pricier. California winemakers have been playing around with Barbera and are producing wines that have big fruit and some spice, and Australia's hot climate has worked for the grape, although the wine doesn't get exported to the States. Barbera appears on almost every decent wine list and in every wine shop, making it an easy go-to red wine.

Because it's fairly high in acid, Barbera only improves with a plate of food alongside it (which isn't surprising, given the famously foodie region where it's grown). Barbera can hold its own against big gamey meats, stews, and hard aged cheeses; it also makes a great pizza wine. Dishes like baked rigatoni, pasta with peas and ham, and even gumbo thrive in the company of Barbera.

50

Cabernet Franc

The wild child of the red varietals, Cabernet Franc (pronounced "kab-er-NAY FRAHNK" and shortened to Cab Franc by most wine geeks) is a blending grape that is trying to show new life as a single varietal. It is the go-to blending grape in Bordeaux, France, where it's blended with Cabernet Sauvignon and Merlot but it's in the Loire Valley that Cab Franc gets the glory: The region of Chinon makes quite a bit of single-varietal Cab Franc in a light, fruity style.

The words *rustic*, *rugged*, and even *savage* could be applied to Cab Franc; with flavors of tobacco, green olive, leather, stewed red fruit, and earth, it's a bit thinner and less tannic than Cabernet Sauvignon. Cab Franc also has a nose that will knock the glasses off your head with herbaceous, spicy plum aromas. (It's also father to the world's best-known red varietal: Cab Franc and Sauvignon Blanc are the parents of Cabernet Sauvignon.)

Long Island, New York, has had great luck with Cab Franc due to the maritime weather, making wines in varying styles from the light, Chinon style to the meaty, herbaceous New World style. California and Washington State have also put out some chewy, mouth-filling examples. You can find a nice Cab Franc for around $20, but the really prized bottles run $50 to $75.

Harmonizing food with Cab Franc depends on the region. With lighter, fruitier Chinon, turn to vegetables and light meats like chicken and pork. Cab Franc from the other regions needs bold flavors to stand up to the punch of the wine. Olives, garlic, and red meat are partners for the bolder styles—even a mushroom pizza will work.

where it's from
France (Bordeaux, Loire), Australia (Coonawarra, Margaret River, Yarra Valley, McLaren Vale); Italy (Alto Adige, Friuli, Veneto); California, Washington State (Yakima Valley, Red Mountain), New York (North Fork, Finger Lakes)

what it tastes like
Raspberries, cherries, plums, violets, bell peppers, green olives, earthy, herbal

producers to look for
Charles Joguet, Philippe Alliet, Yannick Amirault, (France); Crocker Starr, David Cafaro, La Jota, Sirita (California); Moletto (Italy); Colvin Vineyards, Owen Roe, Tamarack (Washington State); Corey Creek Vineyards, Jamesport Vineyards, Millbrook, Shinn Estate (New York)

what you'll pay
$15–$50

dinner party trivia
In the Loire Valley Cab Franc is known as Breton, and in southwest France it goes by the name of Bouchy.

Cabernet Sauvignon

where it's from
France (Bordeaux), Australia (Coonawara, Margaret River, Yarra Yarra), Argentina, Chile (Maipo Valley), Italy (Chianti, Friuli), South Africa, California, Washington State (Snoqualmie)

what it tastes like
Black currants, cassis, eucalyptus, mint, green olives, herbaceous, tobacco, cigar, lead pencil

producers to look for
Chateau Grand Larose, Chateau Pichon Longueville, Chateau de Pez, Chateau Laros-Trintalidon (France); Clos du Bois, Franciscan, Groth, Heitz Cellars, Joseph Phelps, Paul Hobbs, Ravenswood, Smith Madrone, Spottswoode, Vinum Cellars (California); Caliterra, Casa Lapostolle, Domus Aurea, Veramonte (Chile); Penfolds, Rosemount Diamond Label, Voyager Estate, Wolf Blass, Yalumba (Australia); Conte Collalto, Gaja, Torre Rosazza, Zamo & Zamo (Italy); Golden Kaan, Lanzerac (South Africa); Chateau Ste. Michelle, Quelcida Creek, Woodward Canyon (Washingon State)

what you'll pay
$7–$500

dinner party trivia
One of the most expensive wines ever sold was a 1945 Château Mouton-Rothschild, made primarily from Cabernet Sauvignon by the famed French Bordeaux producer. It sold for $28,750 per bottle at a Los Angeles, California, auction.

Cabernet Sauvignon is the regal grape. This is the varietal behind the legendary red wines of Bordeaux, France; the Super Tuscans of Italy; and the grand dames from the Napa Valley. The love child of Sauvignon Blanc and Cabernet Franc, this is a grape that commands respect. Virtually every wine region has planted this grape, resulting in varied styles, although dark berry, cocoa, leather, oak, and herbaceous flavors are always present regardless of the region. These are big, tannic, full-bodied wines—the John Waynes of the red wine world—that practically swagger into your glass. Prounounced "kab-er-NAY so-vihn-YOHN," wine geeks have shortened it to "Cab."

Traditionally Cabs are blended with one of the classic Bordeaux grapes from France (Cabernet Franc, Merlot, Petit Verdot, and Malbec) to give them balance and complexity. (The blend will always be indicated on the label.) The Aussies were the first to blend Cab with Shiraz and it results in magical wines that can be great bargains. Cabs age—that's their thing. With so many tannins these wines need time to soften. Young Cabs are good, tending toward more fruit with more herbaceous flavors, but to really see what this grape can do try one that's at least three years old. As they age, Cabs become elegant and silky, and the flavors soften, producing a huge mouthful of joy. Once you taste a well-aged Cab (five years or older) life will never be the same.

Beef and Cabernet Sauvignon are a long-standing duo, but any grilled meat like lamb will stand up to the wine's myriad flavors. Think big, meaty dishes and skip the fish; the tannins in the wine will just make the fish taste metallic. Cabernet and cow's milk cheeses like Le Moulis and Gouda are a lovely match, and even a mild blue cheese like Gorgonzola will complement this noble red.

FIG and Gorgonzola crostini

serves 6 to 8; makes about 2 dozen crostini

This sweet and savory spread can kick off any party or finish off a wine tasting. If you're expecting a crowd you can easily double or triple the recipe. Serve these with a glass of Cabernet Sauvignon.

1. Preheat the oven to 350°F.

2. Slice the dried figs into quarters. Place them in a bowl with the wine and let them soak for 20 minutes.

3. Meanwhile, lay the bread slices on a baking sheet, brush each with olive oil, and bake for about 8 minutes, until golden brown. Let cool.

4. Drain the figs and transfer them to the bowl of a food processor. Add the cheese, butter, 1 tablespoon of the milk or heavy cream, pepper, and 2 tablespoons of the thyme to the figs and pulse 4 or 5 times, until just combined (the figs should still be chunky). If the mixture isn't soft enough, add an additional tablespoon milk. Taste and add salt if necessary; the cheese is usually salty enough that no additional salt is needed.

5. Spread about 1 tablespoon of the cheese mixture on each slice of bread and top with a pinch of the remaining 1 tablespoon thyme.

note: Crostini can be made up to 1 hour ahead; any more than that and the bread will get a bit soggy.

4 dried Calimyrna figs

1 cup dried black Mission figs

½ cup dry red wine

1 baguette (not sweet), cut on the bias into ½-inch thick slices

Olive oil

½ pound Gorgonzola, at room temperature

2 tablespoons unsalted butter, softened

1 to 2 tablespoons milk or heavy cream

⅛ teaspoon freshly ground pepper

3 tablespoons finely chopped fresh thyme

Salt to taste

53

is for
BLEND

Although many of the world's wines are blends, winemakers from many regions have been playing around with unusual varietals to create blends that are both exciting to sip and food-friendly, which is good news for both our palates and our wallets. While blending wine has been going on for centuries, especially in France, winemakers who aren't faced with legal restrictions on what grape to use (unlike France's complicated laws) are getting on the blending bandwagon to produce interesting everyday drinking wines.

Why blend? Often a varietal is added to another to soften the wine, and sometimes it's done to experiment, accentuate flavors, or to use up excess grapes. While some varietals are better as a solo act, many varietals just aren't tasty on their own (lacking tannin or acidity, for example) and need a little boost. And more often than not, the sum of the parts is better than the individual grapes.

Each country sets the labeling laws about the exact percentage of each varietal in a blend; it's often listed on the back label. Blends are often labeled "white wine", "red wine" or "table wine." In the United States, "table wine" is defined as a wine that is neither fortified nor sparkling, with a 7 to 14 percent alcohol level. Also, American winemakers are increasingly blending grapes with grapes from abroad. Legally a wine can be labeled "American" even if it contains up to 25 percent of grapes grown outside the United States; various countries have different laws regarding how much of the grapes in a blend must be from the country of origin.

Proprietary names are often created by winemakers to brand their blend. Sokol-Blosser's Evolution No. 9, a full-bodied blend from Oregon, reflects the nine white varietals used in the blend. Conundrum is a white blend from California that uses Sauvignon Blanc, Sémillon, Chardonnay, Muscat Canelli, and Viognier from various regions, producing a full-bodied white that instantly pairs with food. (And it's a screw-cap wine to boot.) Another favorite is Bonny Doon's Big House White from California, another screw-cap that's a great everyday wine at under $10. Ménage à Trois White, from Folie à Deaux Winery in Napa, is just as exciting as the name suggests, a blend of Chardonnay, Chenin Blanc, and Sauvignon Blanc. (Folie à Deux makes fabulous red and rosé blends as well.) Two great value blends from Washington are simply called "House White" and "House Red"; winemaker Charles Smith of the Magnificent Wine Co. and K Vintners uses Cabernet Sauvignon, Syrah, and Merlot to make a juicy red blend and also makes a lip-smacking white blend. These are true bargains and worth looking for, in both retail shops and restaurants.

Australia is known for white blends, the most common being Sémillon-Chardonnay blends. This lets the winemaker show off the best of each varietal. For the ABC crowd, these white blends are a chance to see what Chardonnay can do with another varietal. (A few Australia winemakers are playing around with Sémillon–Sauvignon Blanc blends, so keep your eyes out for them. These are medium-bodied wines with great acidity and complexity.)

Red blends are everywhere these days, from every region imaginable. Napa Cabernet Sauvignon–based wines are often blends, and California produces numerous high-end red blends, usually made with the Bordeaux varietals (primarily Cabernet Sauvignon, Merlot, and Cabernet Franc). Italy's Super Tuscans are blends, which surprises many wine lovers. An Italian red blend to look for from the Piedmont region is a complex, bold blend made from Cabernet Sauvignon, Syrah, Merlot, and Nebbiolo called "Monsordo" from wine producer Ceretto.

For reds, look for Qupé's Los Olivos Cuvee from Santa Barbara County, a blend of Syrah, Mourvedre, and Grenache. If you want to spend a little more, look for Flowers Perennial Pinot Noir–Syrah blend, a juicy, spicy blend from Sonoma. Oregon's Penner-Ash Wine Cellars makes a Rubeo blend of Pinot Noir with Syrah. Goats du Roam Red (a play on the French region Côte du Rhône) blends Syrah and Pinotage. Washington is producing a ton of red blends, combining Cabernet Sauvignon, Merlot, Cabernet Franc, and Syrah; they're on the pricey side ($15 to $45) but worth it.

Australia also loves the red blends, the most famous being the GSM blend, a take on the classic Rhône blend, made with Grenache, Shiraz, and Mourvedre. Most are coming from the McLaren Vale and Barossa Valley regions in southern Australia.

A few last notes: The majority of the lower-priced blends are meant for drinking pronto, not sticking in the cellar. On some California blends you might see the word *Meritage*; it's a trademarked name created by the Meritage Association, a group of California vintners who make blends from at least two of the traditional Bordeaux varietals of Cabernet Sauvignon, Merlot, Cabernet Franc, Petit Verdot, and Malbec and the white grapes Sauvignon Blanc, Sémillon, and Sauvignon Vert. To be labeled "Meritage" no single varietal may make up more than 90 percent of the blend. The association came up with the name to distinguish the wines from those labeled "red table wine." *Meritage* is pronounced like the word *heritage*.

Carignan

where it's from
France (Languedoc, Rhône),
Spain, Italy (Sardinia, Sicily),
California

what it tastes like
Black olives, red fruit, herbs

producers to look for
Domaine Bertrand Berge
(France); Coturri Winery, Fife
Vineyards, Frick, Pacific Star
Winery (California)

what you'll pay
$15–$40

dinner party trivia
Carignan is the eighth
most-planted varietal in
the world.

This wine does not go gently into this good night. Most often a blended grape, Carignan (pronounced "care-EEN-ohn") is a brash wine that is high in alcohol, acidity, and tannins. This is the most widely grown grape in France, spreading through the Languedoc, reaching glorious heights in blends from Châteauneuf-du-Pape, but much of it ending up as table wine. It's bottled on its own in California but is usually blended with Grenache and Cinsaut to soften those rough edges; it also forms the basis for much of California's jug wine (Californians spell it Carignane). In Spain it's the second most important grape in the Priorat region, where it's blended with Grenache to make sophisticated, intense wines that sell for $100 and up. Italy latched on to this grape but it mostly appears in blends, primarily from the island of Sardinia, where it's known as Carignano.

This rough-and-tumble varietal just gets better with age, when it softens up a bit. If you can, put them away for five years. Open a bottle of Carignan with spicy pasta puttanesca, roasted pork, grilled sausages, or beef stew.

56

Carmenère

Originally from the Medoc region of France, this grape rose from the dead after phylloxerra, a vine disease that attacks the root system, hit in the 1800s. Traditionally the French threw it into a blend, but Chile led the charge to make a single-varietal wine and Carmenère is now getting the love it deserves. This isn't a sit-around-and-sip wine. Think of it as a crazy two-year-old-with-a-temper wine—there's no taming it. Carmenère (pronounced "car-men-AIR") is a food wine; the bold, ripe flavors of the wine need food to balance it.

In Chile Carmenère led a double life: For years it was thought to be Merlot until DNA testing proved otherwise. Although California's Lake County region has been dabbling in it and Washington State's Walla Walla Valley blends it, it's best to look to Chile for these bad boys. A kick of black pepper and big, bold fruits set this red apart from anything else.

Great deals are to be found for Carmenère; everyday wines start at $6 and top out at $30 for the high-end wines to cellar.

This vivacious wine screams for meat, from smoked meats (duck in particular) to rack of lamb and grilled steak, so uncork a bottle while you're giving in to your carnivorous instincts.

where it's from
France, Chile

what it tastes like
Smokey, dark fruit, pepper, spice, meaty, chocolate, plums, vegetal

producers to look for
Apaltagua, Casa Silva, Concha y Toro, De Martino Legado, Grial, Montes, Santa Ema, Santa Rita, Veramonte, Viña Chocalan (Chile)

what you'll pay
$5–$30 (and up to $70 for the premium Chilean examples)

dinner party trivia
It wasn't until 1994 that a professor of oenology discovered that what was once thought of as Merlot throughout Chile was really Carmenère.

Corvina

where it's from
Italy (Veneto)

what it tastes like
Licorice, smokey, dried cherries, almonds

producers to look for
Alighieri, Allegrini, Bertani, Corte Sant'Alba, Fratelli Tedeschi, Le Ragose, Masi, Romano Dal Forno, Tommasi

what you'll pay
$8–$25 for different categories of Valpolicella

dinner party trivia
The states of Pennsylvania and Virginia are the only other areas in the world where Corvina grapes have been planted.

Two radically different wines from Italy's Veneto region are built on the back of this native Italian varietal: the easy, breezy Valpolicella and the dark, seductive Amarone. (See facing page for more on Amarone.) For both wines winemakers blend Corvina (pronounced "cohr-VEEN-ah") with two other native grapes called Rondinella and Molinara.

There are five classifications of Valpolicella ("vahl-pohl-ee-CHEHL-lah") wine that reflect the style: From lightest to heaviest, they are Valpolicella, Valpolicella Classico, Valpolicella Classico Superiore, Valpolicella Ripasso, and Recioto della Valpolicella. Valpolicella Superiore must be aged longer and has more alcohol and structure than the simple Valpolicella. The Valpolicella Ripasso wines are made by letting the wine go through a second fermentation on the Amarone lees (which, translated to English, means it steals some flavor and color intensity from the Amarone grapes). These are medium-bodied wines with cherry and licorice flavors. (It's said that the cherry trees grown in the region lend the cherry flavors to the wine.) In the past the basic Valpolicella wines have gotten a bad rap with their thin acidic flavors, reminiscent of the carafe wine served in red-checkered-tablecloth Italian restaurants, but producers have been improving the quality.

Recioto della Valpolicella is a sweet version of the wine made with the same process as Amarone, called *appassimento* (see page 124 for more on *recioto* dessert wines), and these are priced anywhere from $20 to $100 a bottle.

At the most basic level, this is another easy red: low in alcohol and tannins with some acidity. Don't age Valpolicellas more than five years. Valpolicella gravitates to virtually any pasta or poultry dish such as roasted chicken as well as lighter dishes like grilled vegetables or the Italian cabbage and bean soup *ribollita*.

AMARONE

Amarone della Valpolicella (usually shortened to Amarone) is one of the secrets of Italian wine. Few people know what it is, or realize the work involved in producing a bottle. This bold yet elegant wine comes only from the Veneto region of Italy and is made with three grapes native to Italy: Corvina, Rondinella, and Molinara. The grapes are picked and then laid on straw mats where, over a few months, they dry into raisins. These dried grapes are then pressed—this is called *appassimento* and results in a concentrated, full-bodied wine with flavors of tobacco, herbs, black cherries, and violets. Amarone (pronounced "ah-ma-ROE-nay") comes from the word *amaro*, meaning "bitter," but the resulting wine is anything but: dry, thick, and rich, with alcohol levels between 14 and 15 percent and distinctive Port-like flavors. Aging just deepens the flavors; ten- to twenty- and even forty-year-old Amarones are not uncommon. It just sings with roasted red meat, stews, or aged cheeses (especially aged Italian cheeses like Asiago and Pecorino Romano or any stinky cheese). Try the traditional Veronese dish of *risotto all'Amarone*, a creamy, deep purple rice dish made with Amarone that will make you weep it's so delicious.

This is a classic example of the phrase "you get what you pay for." Making good Amarone is a laborious process so you'll part with some cash for the best bottles. The best Amarone will set you back at least $40 and up to a few hundred bucks, and this is one wine worth saving your pennies for. Some of the best producers include Allegrini, Alighieri, Bertani, La Casetta, Masi, Serego Tomassi, and Zenato. There are a few lower-end producers, but with Amarone it's almost better to wait and splurge on a good one.

 Dolcetto

where it's from
Italy (Piedmont, Liguria), California

what it tastes like
Ripe, fresh berries such as blackberries, black cherries; plums

producers to look for
Albino Rocca, Aldo Conterno, Azelia d'Alba, Gastaldi, Marchesi (Italy); Bonny Doon, Lucas & Lewellen "Mandolina," Viansa "Athena", Wild Horse (California)

what you'll pay
$10–$20

dinner party trivia
The name *Dolcetto* means "little sweet one" in Italian.

You know your friend, the agreeable one who is polite and smiles a lot but might not be the sharpest tool in the shed? That's Dolcetto (pronounced "dohl-CHET-toh"), a grape that makes pleasant red wines in Italy and California. While Italian Dolcetto is a light, fruit-flavored wine with just the barest hint of bitterness at the end, California versions tend to have brighter fruit and more oak and vanilla flavors. These are reds that should be drunk within three years; any more and the fruit will fade away.

In Italy the most famous Dolcetto is from the town of Alba in the region of Piedmont, labeled "Dolcetto d'Alba." The Italians drink it like water, and for good reason: Dolcetto d'Alba has a bit of acidity but is easy, breezy, and goes down smooth. Dolcetto is more interesting and lively than other light reds like Beaujolais but is still uncomplicated enough for everyday drinking. Some people serve it slightly chilled, but it's perfectly delicious at room temperature.

Dolcetto is the quintessential everyday wine: It won't impose itself on food, and goes great with everything from pasta with meat sauce to pizza, and Chinese takeout. Like Pinot Noir, Dolcetto works with meatier fish and light meats like rabbit and pork. It's also a lovely partner to fontina and mozzarella cheeses.

Gamay

If you've ever found yourself in a wine store in November surrounded by giant signs that announce "Beaujolais Nouveau," then you've met the Gamay grape (pronounced "gah-MAY"). But the light and fruity stuff you're knocking back isn't the true Gamay.

"Real" French Beaujolais (pronounced "boh-juh-LAY") is bright and fruity, but much better than the Nouveau stuff bottled a few weeks before you drink it. What sets Gamay apart from other red varietals is that it's made using the carbonic maceration method. Wine geeks take note: This is a process in which grapes are thrown into the fermentation tank and the grapes ferment inside themselves. The wine is aged from five to nine months before bottling which creates a light, fruity, food-friendly wine.

There are five levels of Beaujolais, from inexpensive to high-end: Beaujolais, Beaujolais Nouveau, Supérieur, Beaujolais-Villages, and Beaujolais Cru (made from one of the ten villages in the region). Beaujolais Cru are the crème de la crème, but even those should be drunk young; aging is not what Beaujolais is about. If you're aiming high and want a Cru, look for wines from the towns of Fleurie, Morgon, and Moulin-à-Vent. (You'll know you're drinking a Cru because it doesn't say "Beaujolais" on the label.)

Beaujolais should be served chilled; even the French serve it chilled. Gamay has never met a food it didn't like. Grilled sausages and roasted vegetable tarts, a simple roasted chicken or Thanksgiving dinner with all the trimmings—pretty much anything goes with Gamay. This is also a great sipping wine, when you're whiling away the afternoon.

where it's from
France (Beaujolais)

what it tastes like
Raspberries, black cherries, violet, pepper, very low tannins

producers to look for
Brunet, Chateau de la Chaize, Georges Duboeuf, Janin

what you'll pay
$5 for the basic Nouveau to $100 for the top level; $15 should get you a nice bottle

dinner party trivia
Beaujolais Nouveau accounts for about a third of the total Beaujolais production. According to French law, it cannot leave the warehouse until 12 A.M. on the third Thursday in November.

61

Grenache

where it's from
France (Rhône), Spain, Italy, California, Australia

what it tastes like
Rustic cherries, black currants, spice, licorice, vanilla, smoke, cigar

producers to look for
Chateau de Beaucastel, Chateau de Saint Cosme, Domaine Les Pallieres (France); Bodegas Tintoalba, Granojo, Marco Real (Spain); Burge Family Winemakers, Clarendon Hills, Rusden, Samuel's Gorge, Yalumba (Australia); Cass Winery, Jade Mountain, Tablas Creek (California)

what you'll pay
$9 for the most basic and $75 and up for French blends

dinner party trivia
Grenache is the world's most widely planted red grape variety.

This fat red grape is grown the world over. It is so hardy it can literally grow everywhere that has plenty of sun, but whether it can stand the heat or just wilts depends on the region. Pronounced "gren-AHSH," it was made famous in France's Rhône Valley, where it's the star player in the wines of Châteauneuf-du-Pape, Côtes du Rhône, and Gigondas, as well as Provençal rosé. These are rustic, rugged wines, with red fruit, spice, and anise flavors. Grenache can be bottled on its own or blended, and blending is often what this alcohol-happy grape needs.

The climate in Spain is perfect for sun-loving Grenache, and it's taken over as the country's lead grape. The Spanish call it Garnacha (as well as Garnacha Tinta) and blend it with Tempranillo to make Rioja as well as the powerful, inky wines of the Priorat region in eastern Spain. In California winemakers often blend it with Syrah, resulting in big, luscious reds that aren't as aggressive as their Spanish counterparts, as well as using it to make rosé. The Rhone Rangers, a wine advocacy group of winemakers in California that grow grapes from Rhône varietals, are trying to improve the reputation and popularity of the varietal, but so far you won't see any stand-alone Grenache coming from the Golden State. (But take one sip of a Grenache blend from a Rhone Ranger producer and you'll be yelling "Yee-haw.") The Aussies have seized on Grenache and are producing more and more every year, making single varietals and blending it with Shiraz and Mourvedre (it's the "G" in the famed intense, spicy, and fruity Aussie GSM blend of Grenache, Shiraz, and Mourvedre; see page 54 for more on blends).

The mighty Grenache needs a full meal to balance it, and the two G's rule this food pairing: Grenache loves the grill. Grilled lamb and steak hold up to the mighty Grenache, although roasted duck or stewed pork and beans would work just as nicely.

Malbec

There are three things to know about Argentina: beef, tango, and Malbec. This chewy, fruity red wine will lure you into a South American mindset. Pronounced "MAHL-beck," the grape has made its home in the dry Argentinian climate and become a star.

Once widely grown in Bordeaux, France, Malbec eventually made it to the Mendoza region, where the tannins are softened and big berry flavors come through. In Argentina both 100 percent Malbec and blends are made; it's often blended with a little Cabernet Sauvignon. In France it's one of the five varietals allowed in French Bordeaux wines (and appears in Bordeaux-style blends from around the world), but these days it's primarily used in the wines of Cahors. In other wine regions, such as California, Australia, South Africa, New Zealand, and Washington, Malbec is used as a blending grape to add a boost of color and tannins to red blends.

Spicy and tannic, big and rich, full-bodied yet soft—these wines don't smack you in the face like the other South American red, Carmenère. Tasty at every price point (although some low-end examples tend to be overoaked), Malbec is the bargain red; you can get a great bottle for $10 and you'll be hard-pressed to find one priced over $30.

Where's the beef? Next to a bottle of Malbec. Beef, which Argentinians consider a major food group, is fabulous with Malbec, as is veal, roast pork, or a plate of grilled sausages. Intense cheeses like Camembert and strong-flavored, blue-veined cheeses play off rich, fruity Malbec.

where it's from
France (Bordeaux, Cahors, Alsace), Argentina (Mendoza), Chile

what it tastes like
Smoke, leather, spice, blackberries

producers to look for
Achaval, Andeluna Cellars, Andes Peak, Bodega Catena, Catena Zapata, Dona Paula, Elsa Bianchi, Luca, Mapema, Navarro Correas, Nieto Reserva, Susana Balbo, Terrazas de los Andes, Trumpeter (Argentina) Luis Felipe (Chile)

what you'll pay
$8–$100

dinner party trivia
A Frenchman named Professor Pouet introduced Malbec to the Mendoza region of Argentina in 1868.

ORGANIC wines

The "O" word is thrown around so much these days that it's hard to see through the hype. Each country sets its own criteria for the label "organic," but in the United States organic wine is defined as wine made from organically grown grapes, which means that no pesticides, fertilizers, fungicides, or herbicides have been used; sulfites are also prohibited. (Although small amounts of sulfites occur naturally, no additional sulfites may be added.) If the wine has sulfites but is otherwise organic, it is labeled "wine made from organic grapes." In addition, some winemakers choose not to use cultured yeasts during winemaking, although this isn't a requirement. France, Italy, and many other Old World wine-producing countries have long histories of organic viticulture and many wines are organic, but they're often not labeled as such.

California started producing organic wines in the 1980s but in the last twenty years almost eight thousand acres have been certified organic, from 117 producers; Mendocino County was the birthplace of the organic wine movement in the United States and currently has the most organic vineyards in California. Bonterra Vineyards, Frey Vineyards, Frog's Leap, Honig Vineyard, Preston Winery & Vineyards, Robert Sinskey, and Grgich Cellars are some of the most well known organic wine producers from California whose wine is widely available. Oregon is also producing plenty of organic and biodynamic wine as well; some top organic producers from Oregon include Amity Vineyards, Sokol Blosser, and King Estate.

Keep in mind, though, that many organic wines aren't labeled as such. There are myriad reasons for this; some wineries don't want to use it as a marketing tool or they don't want to go through the rather intensive certification process. In addition, some of the first organic wines weren't particularly palatable due to inferior vineyard management and winemaking so the reputation of organic wine as "hippie swill" still lingers in some people's minds. Some say there is a taste difference, but that's debatable. Organic wines usually cost more because of the increased labor costs.

Organic wine is often confused with biodynamic wine, but in fact, biodynamic principles are thought to have paved the way for organic farming techniques. Biodynamic (BD for short) wine-making uses the teachings of Austrian anthroposophist Rudolph Steiner, who developed the principles in the 1920s. Steiner believed in looking at things like pest control as part of the entire farm and treating the farm as a whole entity rather than addressing specific problems individually. His teachings incorporate homeopathic treatments to treat vine problems such as mildew, as well as astronomical and astrological considerations, in order to "balance" the vineyard and produce better grapes, the idea being that, in the long run, working with nature is more beneficial than working against it. What may seem like voodoo has been adopted by some of the best wineries in the world.

64

erlot

It's easy to dismiss Merlot as the Chardonnay of the red wine world. Merlot has become the go-to wine for many wine lovers, with its jammy, easy-to-drink qualities. And since the release of the movie *Sideways*, with its Merlot-bashing main character, Merlot has been in the doghouse. Pronounced "mehr-LOW," this varietal gets around: It can grow in virtually any wine region, and it does.

But Merlot isn't the sissy most people think it is. Responsible for the famous Bordeaux wines from France, where it's blended with Cabernet Sauvignon, Merlot is the most widely planted grape in the region. (Ever heard of Petrus? That's almost 100 percent Merlot.) Merlot made a comeback in Italy in the 1990s, and it's planted in several regions there, often blended with Cabernet Sauvignon, Sangiovese, and Syrah. It also makes an appearance in the Super Tuscans. California has been recognized for Merlot since the 1980s, producing very concentrated, lush wines, and it remains a major grape in Napa and Sonoma. Chilean Merlot has more herbaceous, pepper elements and remains one of Chile's most prized grapes. Full-bodied and full of plum and spice flavors, Chilean Merlot is always listed as a value wine. Washington State is also making some fantastic Merlot, very balanced and full of fruit but with nice structure.

Merlot loves anything you throw at it, including pizza and red-sauced pasta to stewed eggplant, roasted duck, and grilled veal chops. Cheese-wise, try Gouda or Provolone; it also contrasts nicely with smoked cheeses such as smoked Cheddar.

where it's from
France, Australia, Chile (Rapel Valley, Colchagua), Italy, California, Washington State, New York (Tuscany)

what it tastes like
Blackberries, blackcurrant, plums, raspberries, spice, chocolate

producers to look for
Chateau Le Conseiller, Chateau Monbousquet, Chateau Pavie, Chateau Simard (France); Carmen, Montes (Chile); Duckhorn Vineyards, Gary Farrell, Matanzas Creek Winery, Ravenswood, Shafer Vineyards (California); Barnard Griffin, Columbia Crest, L'Ecole, Novelty Hill, Northstar (Washington State); Gristina, Lenz (New York); Bollini, Keber, Lupicaia, Mezzacorona (Italy)

what you'll pay
$6–$200

dinner party trivia
Despite the hard knocks Merlot received in *Sideways*, Merlot still makes up about 12 percent of all table wine sold in the United States.

sausage puff pastry bites

makes about 30 pieces

These are pigs in a blanket for grown-ups. The ideal wine-tasting party food, the spicy Italian sausages add bite, but you can use any sausage you like—pork, chicken, or turkey. With store-bought puff pastry these are a breeze to make, and they pair perfectly with Syrah, Sangiovese, or Merlot.

1 pound good-quality fresh sausage (4 sausages; preferably nitrate-free spicy Italian pork sausage)

2 sheets frozen puff pastry, thawed

3 tablespoons grainy mustard

2 tablespoons minced fresh herbs such as rosemary, thyme, and oregano

1 egg, beaten together with 2 tablespoons water

Assorted prepared mustards for dipping

1. Preheat the oven to 400°F.

2. Bake the sausage on a baking sheet for about 30 minutes, until fully cooked, turning once. Let it cool and then cut each sausage in half.

3. Unfold the puff pastry on a floured surface. Brush each sheet with mustard and sprinkle 1 tablespoon of the herbs on each sheet. Cut each puff pastry sheet into quarters.

4. Place one half of each sausage on the edge of a puff pastry sheet and roll it up. Crimp the edges of the pastry, tucking the ends underneath. Repeat with the remaining sausage halves and pastry sheets.

5. Place the sausage rolls, seam side down, on a baking pan and brush the tops with the egg wash.

6. Bake for 20 to 25 minutes until golden brown. Cut them on an angle into 1-inch pieces and serve hot, with several different mustards for dipping.

66

Montepulciano d'Abruzzo

Before you drink this luscious red, first learn to say it: "mon-teh-puhl-chee-AH-noh dah-BROO-zoh." Even if you just point to this Italian varietal on a wine list, though, you'll never be disappointed with these great little red wines. The mountainous region of Abruzzi produces these fruity, soft-textured, easy-to-drink wines. Montepulciano is usually blended with a little bit of Sangiovese. (These are *not* the same wines as Vino Nobile di Montepulciano from Tuscany, which is made primarily from Sangiovese.) Make one your house wine or serve it at your next party. As my sommelier friend Julie says, these are great fruit-forward wines at a steal—usually under $15; what more is there to say?

Break out the pizza and pasta with these wines, including spaghetti with meat sauce and baked pastas like lasagne; they also add a nice contrast to an antipasto platter of salami and pecorino cheese; as well as the local meat of Abruzzi, lamb.

where it's from
Italy (Abruzzi)

what it tastes like
Rich, full-bodied wine with blackberries, cherries, spice, pepper

producers to look for
Caroso, Cataldi Madonna, Citra, Comune di Tollo, Masciarelli, Marramiero, Masciarelli, Valentini, Villa Gemma, Zaccagnini, Zonin

what you'll pay
$8–$15

dinner party trivia
There are four DOC regions in Abruzzi: Contro Guerra, Trebbiano d'Abruzzo, Montepulciano d'Abruzzo, and Montepulciano d'Abruzzo Colline Teramane.

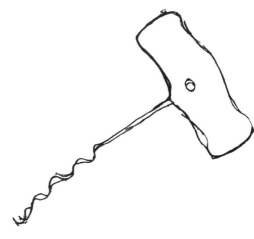

Mourvèdre

where it's from
France (southern Rhône, Tavel, Bandol, Provence), Spain (Rioja Penedes, Alicante); Australia (Barossa Valley), California (Contra Costa County, Paso Robles)

what it tastes like
Blackberries, spices such as cloves and licorice, meaty, leather, gamey, roasted coffee, tannic

producers to look for
Chateau de Beaucastel, Domaine Tempier (France); Barahonda, Bodegas Castano Solanera, Bodegas Olivares Altos de la Hoya, Hecula Yecla (Spain); Bonny Doon Vineyard "Old Telegram," Cline Cellars, Edmunds St. John, Graff Family Vineyards, Preston Vineyards, Tablas Creek (California); d'Arenberg, Hewitson (Australia)

what you'll pay
$8–$25

dinner party trivia
Mourvèdre was originally known as Mataro in California and is sometimes called that in Australia.

With one sip of this edgy, meaty wine you will officially be under the spell of Mourvèdre. Pronounced "moor-VEH-druh," this grape makes wines that are so gamey they're rarely bottled on their own. Instead, Mourvèdre adds an animalistic quality to other fruitier reds; it's often blended with Grenache.

It's a major blending grape in the southern Rhône region of France, and still an important grape in its native Spain. Mourvèdre flourishes in the Bandol region of southwest France; it's the only region in France that requires that the varietal make up at least 50 percent of the wine, producing spicy, almost chewy reds that will alternately shock and thrill you.

Spanish Mourvèdre, where the grape is called Monsatrell, is planted primarily in the Jumilla and Yecla regions. Spanish Mourvèdre are great value reds, full-bodied with tons of fruit and lower tannins than the French examples. Although Mourvèdre was used in bulk wines in Australia in the 1960s, it's now taken off in the Barossa Valley and blended with Shiraz and/or Grenache (it's the "M" in the famous GSM blends: Grenache, Shiraz, and Mourvèdre). This is a grape that gets better with age; these babies can sit in the cellar for ten years or more. Some California winemakers, part of the Rhone Rangers association that works to promote Rhône varietals in California, have started making their own fruity, chocolatey version, in addition to using Mourvèdre as a blending grape.

When thinking about a food pairing, think "strong like bull": roasted meats, game, and strong flavors like olives and garlic go well with this robust red.

CELLARING
wine
What to Keep and What to Drink Pronto

What most people don't realize about wine is that 99 percent of it is meant to be drunk immediately. (And some varietals simply don't age well.) That said, there are plenty of beauties that are worth holding onto.

The reason wine is aged is to bring out complexity. For reds, those harsh tannins soften with age, bringing out new flavors in the wine. Some wines are simply not meant to age, including rosé and many white wines. But there's always the odd bottle that someone brings and you wonder when to open it. Here are some basic guidelines for aging nice wines (that is, those $25 and up in good vintage years), keeping in mind that how the wine is stored makes all the difference:

WHITES
Chardonnay: 4–8 years
Riesling: 8–20 years
Sauternes: 10–15 years up to 60 years

REDS
Amarone: 10–40 years
Barbera, Barolo, and Brunello: 20–25 years
Cabernet Sauvignon: 7–15 years
Pinot Noir: 5–8 years (red Burgundy can age up to 15 years)
Merlot: 5–12 years
Syrah/Shiraz: 10+ years
Petit Sirah: 12–20 years

SPARKLING WINES
Vintage Champagne can be cellared for 20 or more years. Nonvintage sparkling wine should be consumed as soon as possible and cellared for no more than five years.

SHERRIES
The heavier sherries, such as oloroso and Pedro Ximénez, can be cellared, but otherwise they're meant to be drunk immediately, particularly fino and Manzanilla.

PORTS
Vintage Port requires at least a few years of cellaring, but other types of Port are meant to be drunk young.

69

Nebbiolo

The hometown hero of Piedmont, Italy, this grape produces a powerhouse red: It practically assaults your mouth with tannins and acidity. Pronounced "neh-bee-OH-lo," this red varietal is the star behind some famous Italian red wines. (If you've ever had a Barolo or a Barbaresco, you've had Nebbiolo.) Although a few wineries in California have been planting Nebbiolo, they're nothing like the real deal from Italy. There's something about the region—the soil, the climate—that allows Nebbiolo to flourish there like nowhere else in the world.

Barolo and Barbaresco are the names of villages in Piedmont where the most famous Nebbiolo wines are made. These bad boys need to be at least five years old (some say even eight to ten) before you taste them; otherwise they will tackle your taste buds to the ground with their tannins. By law Barolos are aged three years, five years if the label says "riserva," and need at least another few years after that. Barbaresco is a bit more approachable, but that isn't saying much. Knowing the names of good producers is crucial with these wines because the quality varies greatly. This is especially true of Barolo, because the grapes span a wide growing region which affects their flavor and, ultimately, quality. This is the black-leather-jacket-brooding-teenager varietal; when it's good it's very, very good and when it's bad it's ugly. Besides producers, knowing which winemakers make Barolo and Barbaresco in the old style versus the new style—what wine geeks refer to as traditionalists and modernists—makes a difference. To oversimplify it, traditionalists make the wines in the old style, using traditional winemaking methods, while modernists have adopted different, more modern winemaking techniques (shortening fermentation, using oak barrels), which results in two very different wines. Essentially, modernists try to tame the tannins and acidity and bring the fruit forward, while traditionalists allow the tannins to run wild, producing very rustic wine.

Barolos and Barbarescos will set you back at least $30 and up to hundreds of dollars, so it's worth doing some research or finding a wine shop that knows Italian wines before

buying a bottle. (The price reflects both the demand for the wine and the limited supply; only about 9 million bottles of both Barbaresco and Barolo are made every year, and in years with uncooperative weather they're made in limited quantities, if at all.)

A lesser-known area for Nebbiolo is Gattinara, in northern Piedmont. These wines are the entry level to greatness and are much more affordable, usually $18 to $25. Nebbiolo from Gattinara is aged at least four years and often blended with a few other varietals. Because it has so much going on, wines made with the Nebbiolo grape should be decanted before drinking (or at least opened an hour or two before drinking); the air will bring out all the aromas that make it so fantastic.

Plan your meal around these wines. The bigger the food, the better it is with Nebbiolo: Big, rich foods like braised beef cheeks or veal shanks, venison, roasted duck, truffled risotto, roasted mushrooms, and aged cheeses will stand up to this Italian stallion.

TOO SWEET, or not TOO SWEET?

After countless hours talking to wine professionals and sommeliers, every-one begged me to include a little note about sweetness. Sweetness in wine can mean many things. There are sweet wines, when not all of the sugar is converted to alcohol during fermentation, that have actual sugar in them (residual sugar, or RS), and then there are wines that can give the *impression* of sweetness, from the fruity characteristic of the grape or from the oak barrel. (Residual sugar is measured in grams per liter. Wines with a residual sugar level over 45 grams per liter are considered sweet.) Dessert wines contain anywhere between 5 and 30 percent residual sugar. The average palate starts to detect sweetness in wine starting around 1.3 percent residual sugar.

The first wines are in fact sweet but the second set are *dry* wines. Very fruity dry wines can seem sweet, and some oak barrels impart a sweet vanilla flavor. As Master of Wine Mary Ewing-Mulligan points out, fruit aromas and flavors can be sensed in the nose and mouth but sweetness can only be sensed with your tongue. She suggests that if you're not sure whether it's sweetness of fruitiness you're tasting, hold your nose: If the wine is sweet you will taste the sweetness despite not being able to smell anything. Wines with very fruity flavors like Riesling, Gewürztraminer, and Gamay give the impression of sweetness but have less than 1 percent residual sugar, making them dry wines. Winemakers can also *add* sugar, however; sugar is added to cheap jug wines to hide flaws in the wine. (Sugar masks tannins and acidity.) Sugar, like acid, tannins, and fruit, should always be in balance with the other elements.

Petite Sirah

This grape (pronounced "peh-TEET-see-RAH") wins the award for the worst varietal name ever: These wines are anything but petite, and it isn't Syrah (Petite Sirah is a cross between Peloursin and Syrah). Petite Sirah makes big, bold, fruity wines with blackberry and blueberry flavors and lots of spice. Dark purple and with a lot of tannins, Petite Sirah is never put in the corner.

Also known as Durif, Petite Sirah didn't grow well in France but has flourished in the California heat, and that's where it calls home. It's considered a "cult" grape because only five thousand acres are planted in California, but there's no doubt you'll see more of these wines in the coming years. You'll see Petite Sirah bottled on its own, but it's also a major blending grape, joining with Zinfandel, Syrah, and lately with Cabernet Sauvignon, to add color and body to a blend. (Look for "Relentless" from Shafer Vineyard in Napa Valley, a lip-smacking blend of Syrah and Petite Sirah that is phenomenal.) One labeling note: some winemakers spell it "Petite Syrah," despite the fact that the wine is in fact Petite Sirah.

If you can stand to wait, the high acidity allows these babies to age twelve to twenty years, but there are plenty out there that you can drink tomorrow.

These wines yearn for big, rich dishes: grilled meats like lamb, braised short ribs, dark sauces, and grilled or roasted vegetables, especially mushrooms.

where it's from
France, California

what it tastes like
Blueberries, blackberries, pepper, spices such as cloves, tannic

producers to look for
Boeger, Bogle, Clay Station, Concannon, David Bruce, Foppiano, Guenoc, Greg Norman California Estates, Huntington, Ravenswood, Rosenblum, Shafer, Stag's Leap, Trentadue, Turley Vineyards (California)

what you'll pay
$9–$40

dinner party trivia
Recent changes to the Bureau of Alcohol, Tobacco, and Firearms (BATF) rules that govern wine in the United States allow Petite Sirah to be labeled "Durif."

Pinot Noir

where it's from
France (Burgundy), California, Oregon, Australia, New Zealand, Italy (Alto Adige)

what it tastes like
Cherries, red berries, violet, mushrooms, earth, some spice

producers to look for
Armand Rousseau, Domaine de la Romanée-Conti, Domaine Leroy, Faiveley, Jean-Marc Morey, Joseph Drouhin (Côte d'Or, France); Etude, Flowers, Goldeneye, La Crema, Martinelli Winery, Morgan Winery, Pisoni Estate, Siduri (California); Domaine Drouhin, Domaine Serene, Eyrie Vineyards, Firesteed (Oregon); Amisfield, Gypsy Dancer Estates, Huia, Matua (New Zealand)

what you'll pay
$8–$500 (top French red Burgundies like Domaine de la Romanée-Conti cost $1,000 a bottle)

dinner party trivia
Over the course of the twentieth century Pinot Noir has made its way to virtually every wine region in the world.

Pinot Noir (pronounced "PEE-noh-nwahr") is the French poodle of the wine world—prissy, fussy, and downright snotty about where it's from. Winemakers agree that this is one of the toughest grapes to grow, but like most difficult things, all the heartbreak is worth it; the earthy, cherry, velvety tones just sing with every sip. Pinot Noir is rarely blended with any other grape because it's mesmerizing all on its own—blending would just destroy the essence of this varietal.

Pinot Noir produces dramatically different wine depending on where it's grown, and the styles can be split into two categories: Old World and New World. Old World examples include those from France and Italy, and New World includes wines from the United States, Australia, and New Zealand.

France is without question the king of Pinot Noir: When you hear the words "red Burgundy" it means only one thing: Pinot Noir. Supple, earthy wines with aromas and flavors of mushrooms, truffles, and literally the earth are what make these wines so beloved. Explaining the ins and outs of Burgundy would take pages, if not volumes, but here are the basics: There are five major regions in Burgundy, and the Côte d'Or is considered the best. The wines of the Côte d'Or are grouped into four levels that reflect the sophistication (and ultimately the price) of the wine. The Côte d'Or itself is split into two regions, the northern Côte du Nuits and the southern Côte de Beaune. Côte du Nuits produces almost exclusively red Burgundy. If there ever was a reason to splurge on wine it's to taste some great red Burgundy (Premier Cru or Grand Cru) from the Côte d'Or. But "bargain" red Burgundies abound in the Côte Chalonnaise; this includes wine from the appellations of Bouzeron, Mercurey, Rully, and Givry (the fifth appellation, Montagny, makes only white wines).

Italian winemakers are also fond of this grape and call it Pinot Nero, and the wines began to appear in the 1980s. These tend to be young, berry-forward styles from Alto Adige, far from the earthy Burgundian style.

New World Pinots are known for their fruit (mostly cherry) flavors. California loves Pinot Noir and grows it in virtually

74

every region, but Oregon, with a latitude similar to that of Burgundy, is making outstanding Pinots as well.

Because of the work involved in growing and making Pinot Noir, there are few bargains. Low-end Pinots won't really show you what this grape is about and tend to be watery and acidic; expect to spend at least $15 for a good Pinot. One last tip: Wine geeks the world over have shortened Pinot Noir to Pinot, so if you want to sound like a pro just ask for a Pinot.

The ubiquitous pairing of Pinot with any cut of lamb is pure heaven, and game flavors thrive with this grape, including roast duck as well as pork and veal. Stay away from heavy, acidic foods like tomato sauces and beef stews as well as strong flavors like olives and garlicky dishes; they'll overwhelm delicate Pinot. A beautiful, simple quiche or a buttery salmon fillet will delight a Pinot, as will as any type of mushroom: wild or cultivated, roasted, sautéed, or grilled.

moroccan Lamb Tagine

2 tablespoons canola oil (or other neutral-flavored cooking oil)

1 small yellow onion, thinly sliced

1 small fennel bulb, trimmed and thinly sliced

2 large cloves garlic, sliced

1 teaspoon salt

1½ pounds lamb stew meat (boneless lamb shoulder), cut into cubes, at room temperature

2 teaspoons ground cumin

1 teaspoon ground ginger

1 teaspoon ground coriander

¼ teaspoon ground cayenne pepper

About 1 cup water or chicken stock

¼ cup dried apricots, halved

Fresh cilantro or Italian parsley, chopped

A tagine is a Moroccan cooking vessel with a platelike bottom and conical-shaped top used to make simmered stews. You could call it the original slow cooker: Just throw the ingredients in and forget about it for a couple of hours. If you don't have a tagine, use a Dutch oven. Serve this lamb tagine with couscous or basmati rice and open a bottle of Pinot Noir. Syrah is another option; it's peppery and spicy, and the hint of sweet flavors enhances the spices in the dish.

1. Heat 1 tablespoon of the oil in a tagine base over medium heat and add the onion, fennel, and garlic; sauté until just beginning to brown, about 5 minutes. Transfer to a plate.

2. Sprinkle the lamb with ½ teaspoon of the salt. Add the remaining 1 tablespoon oil to the tagine and increase the heat to medium-high. Brown the pieces of lamb in two batches, making sure each piece is browned on all sides, about 4 minutes per batch. Using a slotted spoon, transfer the lamb to a bowl after each batch is browned. Turn the heat to low.

3. In a small bowl, combine the cumin, ginger, coriander, cayenne pepper, and the remaining ½ teaspoon salt.

4. Return the meat to the tagine and add the spices; stir well. Return the onion mixture to the tagine. Add the water and apricots and stir.

5. Cover and cook for 1½ to 2 hours, stirring occasionally. (The meat should be fork-tender and the liquid reduced to a thick sauce.) If the sauce isn't thick enough but the meat and vegetables are done, remove the meat and vegetables to a separate plate and keep simmering the sauce on low until it reaches the desired consistency. As the liquid thickens (after about an hour) you may need to add additional water; add a few tablespoons at a time.

6. Serve hot, with a sprinkling of cilantro or parsley.

Pinotage

This is a red wine that almost defies explanation. Created in South Africa in 1925 by crossing Pinot Noir and Cinsault, Pinotage became the country's unofficial grape. Pronounced "pee-no-TAHJ," it's suffered highs and lows over the years; in some years it was so unpopular that much of the harvest ended up in brandy. Some of that ill will was due to the fact that for years Pinotage producers were plagued by an aroma of paint remover and burnt rubber in the wine that better winemakers have eliminated. This is where it got its reputation as an acquired taste. Added to that, Pinotage is difficult to grow and difficult to describe, with peppery, herbal, and dark berry flavors, with—stay with me here—flavors of banana.

South African winemaking took off only in 1993, after apartheid ended and the various sanctions that were once imposed were dropped, so Pinotage is still finding its place in the American wine market. There are two main styles: light and fruity, and earthy, full-bodied, and tannic. Pinotage is usually made on its own but sometimes blended. South Africa's main growing area for Pinotage is the southwestern region of Stellenbosch. A few California wineries are taking a stab at growing it, but New Zealand is the only country outside of South Africa that has committed to it, although little, if any, makes it to the U.S. market. These are wines that can age, up to ten years.

What to serve with Pinotage depends on the style, and I do mean "serve with." This varietal needs food to show it off. Lighter styles will sit well with grilled fish or even omelettes, while full-bodied Pinotage needs a meat to stand up to it—spare ribs, beef stew, and sausages work perfectly.

where it's from
South Africa, New Zealand

what it tastes like
Bananas, red berries, black pepper, earthy, plums, smokey

producers to look for
Beyerskloof, Boland, Golden Kaan, Kanonkop, Klein Constantia, La Cave, Mooiplaas, Simonsig (South Africa)

what you'll pay
$7–$20

dinner party trivia
Pinotage gets its name from the fact that Cinsault was called Hermitage in South Africa, so the cross of it with Pinot was dubbed Pinotage.

HOW TO stock your "CELLAR," wine closet, or PANTRY

The word *cellar* makes people think of an eighteenth-century chateau with elaborate wine racks and dusty bottles, but don't let that prevent you from putting away some nice bottles of wine. Even if you live in a one-bedroom apartment, you can still stash some bottles to enjoy later.

If you're starting a cellar, remember that the point is to put bottles away to drink in the future. There's no point in buying some nice bottles, getting a wine refrigerator, and then raiding it five months later. Picking which bottle to cellar is important, but constant temperature is the ultimate goal. If a wine is stored in your basement and then moved to a closet that is 70°F, the wine will turn and when you open the bottle it will most likely have gone bad. Wine also doesn't like vibrations, so don't keep the wine near the dryer (or the train tracks). A constant temperature of around 50°F is ideal. Any cold, dark place with a consistent temperature is fine. Humidity is also important; dry air can cause wine to evaporate or come through the cork, causing ullage (the space between

the wine and the cork), which can lead to oxidation, or spoilage. Ideally the humidity should be between 75 and 95 percent.

Store still wines on their side so the corks stay in contact with the wine and don't dry out; sparkling wines can be stored upright because the carbon dioxide in the neck of the bottle prevents air from getting in. If you can build wooden racks, go for it; otherwise choose wooden boxes. Cardboard boxes shouldn't be used for long-term storage because cardboard eventually breaks down and the chemicals in the boxes can affect the wine.

Wine refrigerators are the ideal storage spot if you don't have much room, but there are also wine storage units or lockers in some cities, often located in wine stores. (The added bonus with keeping wine in a storage locker is that you won't be tempted to hit the stash). Skip the kitchen refrigerator as a white wine storage unit; the cold temps will eventually dull the flavors of the wine.

Which wines to store? If you're looking at putting away wine for ten years or more,

78

you're most likely looking at reds such as Cabernet Sauvignon and Cab blends from France and California; reds from the Rhône region of France; Pinot Noir from Burgundy and California; Italian reds such as Nebbiolo and Sangiovese; Spanish reds like Priorat; and dessert wines like Port, Sauternes, and Tokay. You'll spend at least $30 for these wines and up to hundreds of dollars. Some French whites, such as Chardonnay from Meursalt, age beautifully, but generally whites only last about four years. (See page 69 for more information on when to drink what.) If you just want a few special bottles to drink in the next couple of years, look to reds (Zinfandel, Syrah, Australian Shiraz) and whites (Chardonnay from France and Viognier from any region). Expect to shell out $15 and up for these wines.

Your cellar can be anything you want, but if you're geeking out and want a well-rounded selection, try to get one bottle from each of the major wine-producing regions, including those in France, Italy, California, Australia, and Spain; sixty bottles is a good start for a cellar.

Generally you can't taste what you're putting away; you have to rely on recommendations and word of mouth. This is where a reliable wine merchant comes in handy (or a sommelier friend). Occasionally a winery will have library wines—previous vintages of certain wines—that you can taste at the winery to see how they age, or a wine merchant will hold a tasting. If you like what you taste and you have the space, buy two bottles of each. That way you have a back-up in case the wine is corked, and if you love it you'll have another one to drink. If you want to put away a bottle for your kid, buy a magnum, which allows the wine to mature slowly (and makes a dramatic presentation).

If you just want a nice selection of wines to stash in your pantry to drink in the next year, grab a few reds (Pinot Noir, Zinfandel, a Rhône red, and a Cabernet Sauvignon) and a few whites (Sauvignon Blanc, Viognier, Chenin Blanc, and Riesling). Finally, remember to open the bottles! There's no point in amassing lovely bottles and staring at them lovingly. They're meant to be drunk, so make a point to do just that.

Rosé

Pink wine? Before you scoff loudly, remember this: Aromatic, entrancing rosé is one of the most food-friendly wines out there. Not quite a red, not quite a white, it has an undeserved, less-than-stellar reputation.

Rosé, pronounced "roh-ZAY," is French for "pink" or "rose-colored," and it is almost always made from red grapes, including Syrah, Grenache, and Cinsaut and any other red grape a winemaker wants to play around with. What gives it the pink glow? The winemaking process. The skins are removed from the grapes within two to three days, before fermentation, which gives the wine its light pink color. (But it's also why rosés lack the body of most red wines; the tannins are in the skins.)

What started out as a convenience in France—the grapes that didn't make the cut for a red wine were made into rosé—became a national treasure, and France makes more of it than any other country. The French regions of Tavel and Lirac (in the Rhône Valley), Anjou (in the Loire Valley), and Provence, particularly the town of Bandol, are known for their rosé; Tavel is the only region with an AOC dedicated solely to this wine (see page 21 for more on AOCs). But California, Italy, and Spain (where it's called *rosado*) make quite a bit too; a fun Italian rosé (called *rosato*) to try is Cerasuolo, a cherry-colored wine made from Montepulciano grapes. As one winemaker friend points out, rosé is harder to make than either red or white wine because it shows its flaws more readily. So much for a simple pink quaff.

Rosés are dry, fresh, and burst with strawberry and raspberry flavors. Although Americans are apt to think anything pink is sweet, these are not sweet wines. They're crisp wines that make any summer day (really, any day) seem a bit more cheerful. On a sweltering day when you need a glass with more va-voom than a white wine, this is your best bet. Rosé is meant to be drunk pronto, so don't leave them in the back of your closet for years on end. Be sure to serve them slightly chilled.

The labeling of rosé can be confusing; these days the term *vin gris* is used almost interchangeably with *rosé*, although historically it was used for rosé made from Pinot Noir.

However, rosé and vin gris are *not* the same as blush wine, which usually refers to the super-sweet American White Zinfandels.

Because rosé is so food-friendly you can serve it all year long. Virtually every food pairs with dry rosé—garlicky shrimp, vegetable tarts, tuna and avocado burgers, and herbed grilled chicken are a few favorites—but really anything goes. It's also a wine to open if you're serving the Mediterranean flavors of artichokes or anchovy and olive tapenade.

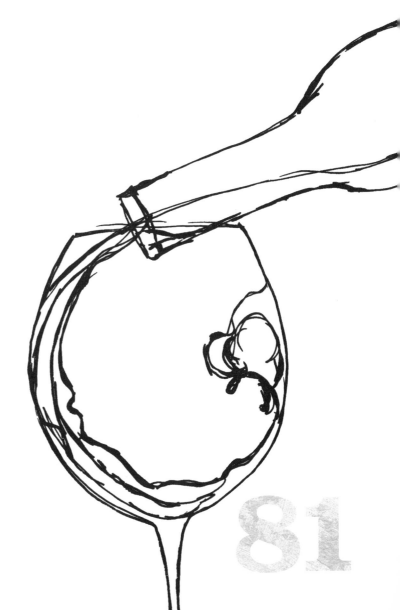

81

Sangiovese

This grape is like a little black dress: It can go from simple to spectacular with just a few accessories. What other grape could go from the most basic Italian Chianti to taking its place in the famed Brunellos (Brunello di Montalcino) from Tuscany?

Depending on where it's from, Sangiovese (pronounced "san-joe-VEH-zay") can be a fairly light bodied sipper or a huge, full-bodied, knock-your-socks-off wine. (Sangiovese also gives hints of orange peel when you sip it even though there's obviously no orange in it.) In Tuscany wines labeled simply "Chianti" will be very light and fruity, while the best Chiantis are labeled "Chianti Classico" and "Riserva." Brunello di Montalcino is comprised only of Sangiovese; these are dark, brooding wines. Sangiovese also appears in Super Tuscans, an unofficial term that refers to nontraditional red blends from Tuscany. The wines feature international grapes such as Merlot and Cabernet Sauvignon that aren't allowed under the Italian DOC and DOCG appellation laws for the region and have a cult following that continues today.

Bargain hunters take note: Vino Nobile de Montepulciano is a region next to Brunello known for value Sangiovese (don't confuse these with the Montepulciano d'Abruzzo grape varietal; in Tuscany Montepulciano is the name of a village). Vino Nobile de Montepulciano are fabulous wines without a hefty price tag.

Not to be left out, California has adopted this grape, producing medium-bodied, deeply fruity wines. Better-quality Sangiovese has been produced since the late 1990s; many of the best ones come from Amador County in the Sierra Foothills. Australia and Argentina have been dipping their toes into this varietal too, producing small amounts of it.

Brunellos can be aged for decades while simple everyday Chianti is meant to be enjoyed immediately.

Bright acidity and low tannins make Sangiovese the ideal tomato wine. With simple dishes like spaghetti and meatballs as well as more sophisticated flavors like grilled lamb, polenta with mushrooms, and Moroccan-spiced chicken, Sangiovese is the wine to pour. Bold cheeses like pecorino bring out the essence of Sangiovese.

Syrah

Want a spicy, fruity wine that's a great value? Grab a bottle of Syrah (pronounced "sih-RAH"), an engaging red wine that dazzles you with layers of deep red fruit and black pepper. It's also a varietal that causes some confusion: Syrah is the same grape as Shiraz but is not the same as Petite Sirah.

With the name game cleared up, here's the skinny on where it's from: Syrah is the darling of the Rhône region of France. These are earthy wines with flavors of dried herbs, and the best come from northern Rhône areas of Hermitage and Côte Rôtie. Because so much is made, Syrah is one of the better French wine bargains and you can't really go wrong with any bottle you choose from there, although the top producers will set you back a pretty penny.

Syrah also flourishes in Australia, California, Washington State, and South Africa, Chile, and Argentina, and each region makes some Syrah worth trying. Australia carved out a niche for itself with Syrah under the name Shiraz (rhymes with *jazz*), which became the country's dominant grape. Shiraz is the primary grape in Penfolds' Grange, Australia's most prestigious red wine. Shiraz from Australia and Syrah from the States taste fruitier and jammier than Syrah from France. South Africa refers to the grape as both Syrah and Shiraz, and those wines are consistently cited as great values. No matter where it's grown, Syrah will have elements of black fruit (blackberries and prunes), coffee, and the beloved black pepper. Just how spicy it is, however, relates directly to where it's grown: The cooler the climate, the spicier the Syrah.

Bold flavors and any herb on the planet suit Syrah just fine; dishes from Korean short ribs and barbequed meats to roasted game, rich stews, and cheeses like Parmesan and aged goat cheese will come to life with a glass of Syrah.

where it's from
France (Rhône), Australia, California (Santa Barbara, Sonoma), Washington State, South Africa, Chile, Argentina

what it tastes like
Black pepper, red fruits, rustic, smoke, coffee, leather, roasted meat, bacon

producers to look for
Alain Graillot, Chapoutier, E. Guigal, Michel Ogier (France); K. Climicky & Sons, Penfolds, Thorn-Clarke, Wolf Blass, Wyndham (Australia); Copain, Delicato, Echelon, Michel Schlumberger, Novy Wines, Peay Vineyards (California); Chateau Ste Michelle, Columbia Winery, Covey Run, Mark Ryan, Three Rivers Winery (Washington State); Alta Tierra, La Ronciere, Luis Felipe (Chile); Bodegas Salentein, Luca, San Juan (Argentina); Brampton, De Trafford, Rudi Schultz (South Africa)

what you'll pay
$7–$100 for the crème de la crème

dinner party trivia
What makes the wines from Côte-Rôtie so expensive is due to both the small number of vineyards and the steep hillsides of the region: During harvest pickers must carry wooden crates of grapes on their shoulders up and down the hills.

83

SPICY VEGGIE SAUTÉ

serves 4 to 6

3 tablespoons extra-virgin olive oil

1 yellow onion, chopped

2 teaspoons salt, or more to taste

1 teaspoon freshly ground black
    pepper, or more to taste

3 large cloves garlic, chopped

6 carrots, cut into 2-inch lengths

¼ cup piquillo peppers, sliced
    (jarred roasted red peppers
    can be substituted)

2 cups small cauliflower florets
    (from ½ head cauliflower)

1 cup sliced mushrooms

½ eggplant, cut into 1-inch cubes

1 teaspoon red chile pepper
    flakes, or to taste

1 teaspoon paprika

1 (14-ounce) can diced tomatoes,
    with juice

1 (14-ounce) can chickpeas,
    drained

2 teaspoons fresh oregano,
    minced

2 teaspoons fresh marjoram,
    minced

2 teaspoons fresh Italian parsley,
    minced

Lemon wedges, for serving

If you need inspiration for vegetables, or just have a lot of vegetarian friends, whip this Mediterreanean sauté up on a weeknight. Serve it over couscous, orzo pasta, or polenta for a complete meal. A Syrah (and the fruity Shiraz) stands up to the mild spiciness of the dish, as will most red blends.

1. Heat the olive oil in a large sauté pan and add the onion, salt, and pepper. Sauté for 5 minutes and then add the garlic. Cook for 2 minutes, then add the carrots, piquillo peppers, cauliflower, mushrooms, and eggplant and stir. Add the pepper flakes and paprika and stir to incorporate. Add the tomatoes and stir.

2. Turn the heat to low, cover, and simmer for 30 minutes, stirring occasionally, until the vegetables are soft. Add the chickpeas and herbs and cook for 5 minutes. Taste and season with salt and pepper as needed.

3. Serve with lemon wedges (the lemon perks up the flavors).

This dish tastes better the longer it sits, so you can make it up to 2 days ahead. It's delicious served hot or cold.

84

Tempranillo

Pronounced "tem-pra-NEE-yoh," this grape put Spain on the world wine map. Aside from flamenco and sherry, *Rioja* is the word most often associated with Spain. Tempranillo is the grape behind the most famous Spanish wine, Rioja, and Spain produces more Tempranillo than any other country. This is a lighter red, with higher acid and lower alcohol, making it a great food wine. (Considering how much the Spaniards love their food, this shouldn't be surprising.)

Spanish winemakers love the oak, so examples from Spain will have vanilla flavors from their time in oak barrels. Australia, Argentina (where it's spelled *Tempranilla*), South Africa, and California are also joining the Tempranillo party, with a handful of producers planting the grape. Australia in particular has been planting the varietal in about half of their wine regions and blending it with Grenache and Syrah in a medium-bodied, fruity style. Tempranillo is often blended with Grenache (called Garnacha in Spain), and/or Cabernet Sauvignon to give it a deeper color and more intense flavor.

In Spain Tempranillo is labeled according to region, with Rioja and Ribera del Duero the most well known areas, but the up-and-coming regions of Navarra, Somontano, and Toro also produce some great Tempranillos. The label will also indicate the quality; look for "DO" or the higher-quality "DoCa" on the label. (See page 21 for more on Spanish wine labels.) You can put these wines away for few years if you're into cellaring; they definitely get more complex with age.

Because Spain is a country dedicated to food, Tempranillo is a natural match for a wide range of flavors. This is a food wine to be served with dishes like grilled leg of lamb or pork, duck confit, smoked meats including any type of sausage and charcuterie, mushroom risotto, sheep's cheese, Manchego cheese (a hard Spanish goat's milk cheese), and, of course, paella.

where it's from
Spain (Rioja, Ribera del Duero, Navarra), Portugal (Duoro Valley), Australia, Argentina, South Africa, California

what it tastes like
Vanilla, plums, prunes, cherries, spice, herbs, earth, leather

producers to look for
Bodegas Alejandro Fernandez, Cune Imperial, Marqués de Caceres, Martinez Bujinda, Montecella Reserva, Montecillo, Pesquera, Protos, San Vincente (Spain); Familia Zuccardi, Mapema (Argentina) Clos du Bois, Gundlach Bundschu (California)

what you'll pay
$7–$50

dinner party trivia
In Spain Tempranillo is known by a different local name depending on where it's grown: In Catalonia it's called Ull de Llebre; in Castile–La Mancha and Madrid it's known as Cencibel, and in Castile and Leon it goes by Tinto Fino and Tinto del Pais.

85

ALTERNATIVE
wine closures

Just a few years ago a wine lover would have run screaming at the sight of a twist-off, a boxed wine, or a fake cork. Here's the truth behind the packaging.

Screw-Caps: Remember those gum ads that said nine out of ten patients who chewed gum preferred their brand? The same phrase can be used for screw-caps. Nine out of ten wine-makers will tell you that screw-caps are better closures because they are the best way to prevent corked wine. But convincing consumers—and even some wine industry professionals, retailers, wine buyers, and sommeliers—of this is another matter. Those forward-thinking Aussies and Kiwis were the first to bottle large amounts of wine under screw-cap, and slowly other wine regions are getting on board. You'll see wine from the States and even a few from France with screw-cap closures. While many bemoan the lack of ritual and the loss of tradition, screw-caps let you close the wine back up for a few days and eliminate the need for a corkscrew. The jury is still out on aging wines in screw-cap bottles but even so, wines at all price points are being unscrewed, so get used to it.

Synthetic Corks: Plastic corks made their debut in the early 1990s. Wineries have adopted them because they're cheaper than real cork (high-end corks can cost up to 75 cents each) and there is no risk of cork taint. They're used for wines that are meant to be drunk in five years or less because their less-than-perfect seal doesn't let the wine age. Another downside is you can never get those suckers back in once you've uncorked a bottle. Bottom line: If you see a bright purple plastic cork emerge from your bottle, it just means it's a drink-it-now kind of wine.

Boxed Wine: Don't laugh. Wine in a box, sometimes called cask wine, is something you're going to see more of; the premium 3-liter size is one of the fastest-growing segments in the American wine market. The Aussies have "bottled" wine in boxes for years, but in the States boxed wine was usually low-end cooking wine.

There is still some scary boxed wine out there, but premium wines are starting to take over. Premium boxed wine is packaged in pouches hidden inside 3-liter boxes, which are the equivalent of four bottles. (Premium versus "regular" boxed wine lies in the size: Premium boxed wines are in 3-liter boxes and priced $15 to $25, while the 5-liter boxes are the lower-end wines to pass on.) In addition to 3-liter boxes, a few good wine companies are packaging their wine in 1-liter Tetra Paks, similar to what milk and juice come in. These 1-liter packs are equal to six glasses of wine and the packaging is eco-friendly; they're about $7–$10 a pop. Besides being convenient—you can drink what you want and the wine stays fresh for up to a month—the value is fantastic: The savings in packaging and shipping for the wineries are so considerable that they can pass the savings along to you. Boxed wines are also perfect if you're heading somewhere that doesn't allow glass, like an outdoor concert, a boat, or a poolside bash. Some tasty boxed wine to look for: Tindindi Cellars, Hardy's, and Banrock Station from Australia; French Rabbit and DTOUR from France; Black Box, Three Thieves Bandit, Trove, Delicato Vineyards' Bota Box, Fisheye Wines, and Wine Cube (a brand only available at Target stores) from California; and Washington Hills from Washington.

Zinfandel

where it's from
California

what it tastes like
Jammy, raspberries, spice, black licorice, medium- to full-bodied

producers to look for
Bella Oaks, Fife, Peachy Canyon, Rabbit Ridge, Ravenswood, Rosenblum Cellars, Ridge Vineyards, Seghesio Family Vineyard, Turley Vineyards (California)

what you'll pay
$7–$50

dinner party trivia
Zinfandel was the only grape widely grown in California during Prohibition. During Prohibition winemaking was limited to wine used as medicine, food flavoring, or as sacramental wine, but home winemaking was exempt. So Zinfandel grapes were shipped to "home winemakers" across the country.

Zinfandel could be called the patriotic grape. American winemakers claim it as their own, even though DNA testing proved that it originated on the Dalmatian Coast in Croatia. (Wine geek note: It's referred to as "Zin.") The Italians have a genetically similar grape called Primitivo, grown mainly in the southern region of Puglia, but there's much debate as to whether it's the same grape as Zinfandel; Italian Primitivo is more rustic and spicier than American Zins. This is a show-off grape, with big, bold, flavors of cooked fruit (like inhaling spoonfuls of berry jam) and spice. They pack a punch, coming in at around 15 percent alcohol, and they'll stain your teeth for days on end. One Napa Valley producer, CrauforD, makes a "Kilt Lifter" Zinfandel, and that pretty much says it all: These wines swoop in and knock you off your feet.

Spain, Australia, and Argentina also grow it but it the wine isn't exported to the United States. California is really the leader of the Zin club, where it can be found in every grape-growing region; some of the best Zins come from Napa, Sonoma, and Mendocino. You can put a Zin away for up to ten years but most are drinkable right off the shelf.

The acidity and fruit in Zin makes it the perfect pairing for tomato sauce, grilled meat (including hamburgers), spare ribs, slow-cooked veal shanks, stuffed roasted peppers—anything that needs a strong wine to match it. There's nothing shy about this grape, so it needs an equally bossy food to show its stuff. Don't pair these wines with spicy food; it will only make the food seem even spicier.

GRILLED SKIRT STEAK WITH HERB CHIMICHURRI

serves 4 to 6

Skirt steak is a grill-friendly cut that needs quick cooking so that it doesn't toughen up. The sauce is inspired by the Brazilian chimichurri, a chunky sauce made from herbs and garlic. The zing of the sauce brings out the spice in a Zinfandel, matches a young Cabernet Sauvignon, and complements a bottle of Sangiovese.

1. About 30 minutes before cooking, remove the steak from the refrigerator.

2. Heat the grill to high (or place a grill pan over high heat). Cut the steak into 4 equal pieces. Rub the meat 3 tablespoons of the oil and season generously with salt and pepper.

3. Make the chimichurri: In a food processor, pulse the herbs, garlic, ½ teaspoon each of salt and pepper, and the pine nuts. (You can also use a mortar and pestle.) With the food processor on, slowly add the remaining ½ cup oil, being careful not to overprocess; the sauce should be chunky, not runny. (If it seems too dry, add more oil.) Season to taste with salt and pepper. The sauce can be made 2 days ahead. Cover and refrigerate; bring to room temperature before serving.

4. Grill the steak for about 2 minutes on each side, turning once; if the pieces are very thin you may only need to cook them for only 1 minute, and if they're thicker it may take up to 4 minutes per side. (If you're using a grill pan, heat 2 tablespoons canola oil in the pan until smoking. Add 2 pieces of steak at a time, searing it for 2 minutes per side.) Remove the steak from the grill and cover loosely with foil.

5. Let the meat rest for 5 minutes, then cut on the bias into ½-inch thick slices against the grain. Serve each portion with a spoonful of the sauce.

1½ pounds skirt steak

About ½ cup plus 3 tablespoons olive oil

Salt and freshly ground black pepper

1 cup fresh basil, washed and stemmed

1 cup fresh Italian parsley, washed and stemmed

½ cup fresh mint, washed and stemmed

3 medium-sized cloves garlic, roughly chopped

1 cup pine nuts

BUBBLY

WHERE YOU FIND WINE,

you usually find bubbles. Somehow wine can become even more complex, regal, and interesting when it arrives with a mouthful of bubbles. But if you thought making wine was a lot of work, you don't know what you're in for. Nature and very skilled winemakers join forces to create one of the most magical types of wine. Virtually every wine region in the world makes its own bubbly, ranging from deep and rich to flighty and forgettable. Whether you're celebrating, sipping, or enjoying a meal, there's a sparkling wine for you.

First, the basics: Not all sparkling wine is Champagne. Bubbly labeled "Champagne" can only be made in the Champagne region of northeast France using specific methods and grapes. Everything else, and I mean everything, should be referred to as "sparkling wine." (The French have been trying to get an official rule about this, and a few countries signed an informal agreement, but so far the term *Champagne* can be co-opted by other regions. The Americans never signed, so some of their sparklers are labeled "champagne," usually, but not always, with a lowercase "c.")

Second, not all sparkling wine is made with white varietals; both red and white varietals are used. (Wine only gets its color from the skins of the grapes; this means that white wine can be made from black grapes if the juice comes in minimal contact with the skins.) The varietals used in sparkling wine include Chardonnay (Champagne and sparkling wines); Pinot Noir (Champagne and sparkling wines); Pinot Meunier (Champagne and sparkling wines); Prosecco (Italian Prosecco); and Xarel-lo (Spanish Cava). Finally, there are several types of Champagne: *blanc de noirs*, *blanc de blancs*, and rosé. *Blanc de noirs* is made from the red grapes Pinot Noir and Pinot Meunier; *blanc de blancs* uses only Chardonnay; and rosé contains only Pinot Noir and Chardonnay. In Champagne *blanc de noirs* is extremely

92

rare; it's made more often as a sparkling wine. (For more details on the differences among the types, see Champagne Terms, page 111.)

Depending on the region, sparkling wine is made by three or more different methods. The basic premise for any sparkling wine is that when the fermentation occurs in a closed vessel the carbon dioxide, created by the yeasts, becomes trapped in the wine and forms bubbles. This occurs through a second fermentation which converts the still wine into bubbly. The second fermentation has to be created by the winemaker by the addition of sugar and yeast; it doesn't occur naturally.

CHAMPAGNE AND SPARKLING WINE METHODS

Methode Champenoise

The true method of producing Champagne, *methode champenoise*, is expensive and time-consuming. A brief summary of the process: The wine goes through its first fermentation, and the winemaker creates his or her base wine from the different grape varieties, often including some reserve wine from a previous vintage. The key is blending—*cuvée* is the French word for "blend"—and the winemaker must be a master blender, utilizing different grapes from different years and different vineyards. The base wine is put in the bottle, the bottle is sealed, and the wine then goes through a second fermentation in the bottle. This can take about a year and up to three years, and during this time the bottles are turned (a process called *remuage*, or "riddling," developed by Veuve Clicquot) so that the solid lees travels to the neck of the bottle. The lees is flash-frozen in the bottle and then

expelled, a dosage (sugar dissolved in reserve wine) is added to the sparkling wine just before final corking, and then the bottles are corked and labeled. This method is also called the traditional (*traditionnelle* in French) or classic method.

Several regions besides Champagne use this method, including some California sparkling wine producers and Cava producers in Spain. Why the big fuss over true Champagne? The Champagne region has the perfect climate for producing high-acid grapes, which are a main ingredient in making great Champagne, as well as a history of making truly incredible wines. In Champagne producers are called "houses" and each house develops a style, based on the weight of the wine in the mouth, and this style becomes recognizable once you taste Champagne from a few different houses. The top Champagne houses produce *cuvée de prestige*, the most famous being Moët & Chandon's Dom Perignon and Louis Roederer's Cristal.

Charmat Method

This is the less-expensive method used to make some sparkling wines. The grapes are put in stainless-steel tanks along with yeast and sugar, sealed, and allowed to ferment, and after the second fermentation in a tank and the addition of some sweetness, the sparkling wine is bottled. These sparklers aren't aged and are meant to be drunk the moment they're released. This is also called the bulk method or tank method.

Carbonation

A third method that is only used for very cheap sparkling wine is when gas is added to a wine to make it sparkling. This is carbonation, the same process used to make soda fizzy, and must be indicated on the label. Bubbly made this way has large bubbles that disappear quickly.

94

CHOOSING a BUBBLY

Many factors determine the quality of sparkling wine, including the size of the bubbles, balance, and texture. The size of the bubbles (fine versus fat) set sparklers apart. True Champagne has the smallest bubbles, and the smaller the bubbles, the better the wine. (If the bubbles are smaller, there are more of them in the glass, and when they explode on the surface of the wine they release all the flavor and aroma of the wine.) The temperature of the cellar and the length of aging affect the size of the bubbles, while the number of bubbles is determined by the proteins in the grape varietals, among other technical factors.

In addition to the quality, before you buy a bottle of bubbly consider the house style. House style is usually described by the body of the wine (light, light to medium, medium, medium to full, and full) and is determined by the type of varietal used and particular vineyards. For example, light-style Champagne has more citrus flavors and is light as air in the mouth; producers known for their light style include Laurent-Perrier and Taittinger. A Champagne made in the full style will taste of toasted bread and vanilla, and have a mouth-filling texture, almost like eating a buttery brioche; producers include Bollinger, Gosset, Krug, and Veuve Clicquot. Medium-bodied are a combination of both; well-known producers include Deutz, Charles Heidsieck, and Mumm.

There are many wonderful, earth-shattering Champagne producers; the top ones include Krug, Billecart-Salmon, Dampierre, Taittinger, Gosset, Charles Heidsieck, Salon, and Veuve Clicquot. High-quality Champagne doesn't come cheap; a bottle usually starts at $30 and can run into the hundreds of dollars for vintage Champagne. In addition to the big names—there are over twelve thousand Champagne houses in the region—there are also dozens of small producers, what you could call the artisanal producers. Most of these producers, which account for less than 2 percent of all Champagne imports in the United States, appear only in top restaurants, both by the glass and in the bottle, and in specialty wine stores. A few small producers worth seeking out are Alain Robert, Bruno Paillard, Larmandier-Bernier, Pierre Gimonnet, and Pierre Moncuit.

continued on page 98

ORDERING WINE in a RESTAURANT

without taking out a second mortgage (or looking like an idiot)

Take a minute to look over the list and get the lay of the land. Don't be pressured by a hovering sommelier or waiter.

Ask the sommelier for a recommendation. They're there to help, not torture you. Really.

Wines by the glass: If you are having a light fish dish and your dining companion is having pizza, order wines by the glass. Many restaurants are upping their wine by the glass programs, with ten or twelve (and sometimes up to fifty wines) open for you to taste. That said, if you and your friend(s) are ordering three glasses of the same wine, buy the bottle—it will be cheaper. Or order half-bottles; they're a great option for sharing. Remember that in many states you can take an unfinished bottle of wine home with you; ask your server or the restaurant manager if they participate (it's voluntary). The laws vary from state to state, but "Merlot to Go" laws exist in thirty-one states.

Choose your price range and stick to it; you don't have to be bullied into overspending. The best way to get a bang for your buck is to try lesser-known varietals and regions (the ABC rule!). Instead of a Napa Chardonnay you'll get much more for your money if you order a Chenin Blanc from South Africa or a Sauvignon Blanc from Chile. And head for the middle: Most often the mid-priced wines are great values and not extreme in terms of flavor (they will exemplify the wine style and won't be wacky—that is, they won't scare off any wine newbies in your group). One last note: The cheapest wine on the menu is not necessarily the worst wine! Many restaurants (and most wine-loving restaurants) put lower-priced wines on the list to make it more affordable.

96

If the wine you choose is out of stock, which happens more often than not, ask for a similar wine in that price range.

Corkage: Restaurants usually charge a fee if you bring your own wine. The corkage fee covers glassware and service, but before you think this is a way to save money, ask what the corkage fee is. Many restaurants charge such a high corkage that it will cost you more than the bottle. If you do go to the trouble to bring your own bottle, don't choose the $7 grocery store special—make it a nice one. Bringing an inexpensive wine, or a wine that is already on the restaurant's wine list, makes you look cheap and just isn't done. Of course, corkage isn't the same as BYOB (bring your own bottle, usually offered by restaurants that don't have a liquor license). If a restaurant has a BYOB policy, bring whatever bottle you want.

Pricing: Wines in restaurants are more expensive than they are in wine shops. End of story. You're paying for the privilege of sitting and enjoying the bottle. But that doesn't mean you can't get a few good deals. And quite often restaurants carry bottles that you won't see in retail shops, so the experience is worth it.

Sending a bottle back: Unless a wine is corked (smells and tastes like an old musty cellar), you can't send back a bottle of wine just because you don't like it. Some restaurants will offer tastes of the wine if they sell it by the glass, but usually you have to take it on faith that the wine will be to your liking. If you do think the wine is corked, ask the sommelier or server to try it; most good restaurants will replace the bottle with no questions asked.

97

continued from page 95

Most Champagne is sold in standard-sized 750mL bottles but a few smaller formats are also available. The tiny half bottles, 375mL or splits, are fun options, especially Neibaum-Coppola's "Sofia" sparkling wine sold in individual cans and Pommery's "Pop" Champagne in 187mL, single-serving bottles. But if you're planning to keep them for a while, buy bubbly in 750mL (or larger) bottles.

sweetness Levels

The sweetness level of a Champagne or sparkling wine is always indicated on the label; Brut is the most common.

EXTRA BRUT OR BRUT NATURALE: Bone dry

BRUT: Dry. This is the typical style of Champagne, with no sweetness.

SEC: Still very dry but with a hint of sweetness.

DEMI-SEC: This means half dry, although the wine will be fairly sweet.

DOUX: Sweet; also known as rich, this wine is the sweetest you can get in Champagne and contains over 5 percent sugar. It's very rare.

Dungeness crab Dip

serves 6 to 8

This creamy dip accentuates the flavor of buttery, delicate Dungeness crab. If you can't get Dungeness, blue crab works fine; it will just have a more assertive crab flavor. Serve this sinful dip with sparkling wine; a yeasty, rich Champagne would be divine.

1. Preheat the oven to 350°F. Butter a 10-ounce baking dish (or any large ramekin).

2. In a large bowl, combine the breadcrumbs and the half-and-half and set aside to soak.

3. Heat the 2 tablespoons butter in a large sauté pan, add the green onions, and sauté for 3 minutes. Add the celery and for cook 4 minutes more.

4. Add the parsley, lemon juice, yogurt, cheese, dry mustard, cayenne pepper, paprika, salt, and pepper to the bread mixture and mix gently with a spatula. Add the onion–celery mixture and mix gently, then fold in the crabmeat. Taste and add salt if necessary; crab can be salty so it's best to taste for salt after adding the crab.

5. Transfer the crab mixture to a buttered baking dish and bake for 20 to 25 minutes, until warmed through and lightly browned. Serve warm, with crackers or baguette slices.

½ cup fine breadcrumbs

½ cup half-and-half

3 green onions, green and white parts, finely chopped

2 tablespoons unsalted butter (plus additional for greasing the dish)

3 tablespoons fresh Italian parsley, minced

2 stalks celery, finely chopped

1½ tablespoons freshly squeezed lemon juice

⅓ cup plain whole-milk yogurt

½ cup Parmigiano-Reggiano, finely grated

1 teaspoon dry mustard

¼ teaspoon ground cayenne pepper

¼ teaspoon paprika

¼ teaspoon salt, or more to taste

¼ teaspoon freshly ground black pepper

1 pound fresh lump crabmeat, preferably Dungeness, picked through to remove any shells

Crackers or baguette slices, for serving

99

SPARKLING WINE FROM AROUND THE WORLD

Cava Spain's answer to Champagne is Cava (pronounced "KAH-va"). Using local grapes, primarily Xarel-lo, Macabeo, and Parellada, Cava is made with the *champenoise* method in the Penedés region. By law they must be aged a minimum of nine months. These are lively, fruity sparklers that are fantastic bargains, with most selling for around $10. Some producers do use Chardonnay and/or Pinot Noir to make Cava, but only a few of the best. They should be drunk young. Look for Cava from Cristallino, Freixenet, Segura Viudas, and Parellada.

Crémant d'Alsace Pronounced "kray-MAHNT dahl-SASS," this is sparkling wine from the Alsace region of France. The *champenoise* method is used to vinify a handful of approved varietals, including Pinot Gris, Pinot Noir, Riesling, Pinot Blanc, and/or Chardonnay. French law requires that it be aged a minimum of nine months; they cost around $14. Alsatians often use Crémant d'Alsace in cocktails. The term *crémant*, which means "creaming" in French, is used to describe sparkling wine from France made outside the Champagne region. Other Crémant includes Crémant de Bordeaux (made from Sémillon, Sauvignon Blanc, and Ugni Blanc), Crémant de Bourgogne (made from Pinot Noir, Chardonnay, and Pinot Gris, among others), and Crémant de Loire (made primarily from Chenin Blanc).

Prosecco The Italian bubbly is Prosecco (pronounced "proh-SECK-oh") and is made in the Veneto region from the white Prosecco grape in the Charmat method. Although several sparkling wines are made in Italy, including Moscato d'Asti, Asti Spumante, and Brachetto d'Acqui, Prosecco is usually dry with flavors of green apples, although there are sweet styles. The very best Proseccos are labeled "Superiore di Cartizze" and come from a subzone within Valdobbiadene. Good producers include Mionetto, Zardetto, Nino Franco, and Bisol; they cost between $8 and $20.

continued on page 106

HOW TO STORE leftover WINE

(if there is any)

Because of oxygen, wine "goes bad" once you pull the cork. Once oxygen hits the wine, it starts to, well, oxidize. You can slow down the process, but you'll never completely reverse it. That said, you can keep a bottle for a few days using a few different tools (and overnight just by sticking the cork back in). After a week, it's time to toss it. Here are a few ways to preserve an open bottle.

Wine gas: Wine geek alert: Inert gas will keep your wine fresh for days. (Inert gas is essentially pure air that contains no oxygen, and it prevents oxidation of the wine.) The two most common brands, Wine Life and Private Reserve, come in cans that feel empty. It feels empty because the gas inside is lighter than air and replaces any oxygen left in the bottle with the gas, preserving the wine. Just spray and recork and the wine will stay fresh for at least a few days and up to a week (and some say up to a month). (You can find wine preserver in wine shops and online for around $10 a bottle; one bottle should be good for about a hundred uses.) If you want to be fancy about it, there is a "wine preservation steward" that replaces the oxygen in the bottle with argon gas that sells for around $200; it's about the size of a coffee maker and keeps wine fresh for up to three weeks.

Wine vacuum: A vacuum pump draws out any oxygen in the bottle and seals it, preserving the wine for two to three weeks. You just place a stopper over the top and pump out the oxygen. They cost anywhere from $10 to $50. (But a vacuum won't work on sparkling wines.)

Half bottles: An easy and cheap way to preserve your wine is to pour it into half bottles (375ml), eliminating excess oxygen. My winemaker friend swears by it.

The refrigerator: Several winemakers I know stick half-empty bottles of wine in the fridge, both whites and reds. It slows down the deterioration of the wine. Just pull the reds out about an hour before you want to finish the bottle.

Bubbly: Obviously sparkling wine poses additional problems given the carbon dioxide involved (you will never revive those bubbles), but a cheap Champagne stopper will keep it overnight (and you can cook with leftover sparkling wine; it makes a great wine sauce). An old wives' tale is to stick a silver spoon (handle down) in the mouth of the bottle and put it in the fridge.

101

HOW TO BUY wine WISELY at retail

Cases are your friend. Virtually every wine shop offers case discounts, and mixed cases are almost always welcome. If you find yourself buying wine more than once a week, buy a case—you'll save time and moola.

Some states allow grocery stores to sell wines. Many stores are able to offer great deals because their size gives them more buying power with the bigger wine brands. Trader Joe's, for example, handles a lot of wine that is "leftover" or overflow inventory that wine companies want to get rid of, and they also have leveraged buying power. This can mean good deals for you. But in general most supermarket prices are higher than those you'll see in the average wine store because you're paying for convenience.

Get to know your local wine merchant and patronize his or her shop. Establishing a relationship with a wine merchant is a great way to get deals, insider tips, unusual wines, and reliable wine advice. Smaller retailers also often hold tastings, which is a great way to explore new wines. Service is what sets good shops apart, and often the smaller stores will specialize in certain types of wine. Stay clear of the wine merchant who always steers you to the most expensive bottle; while some wines are expensive, there are great wines available at all price points.

Buying wine online: Online wine purchases can be hit or miss. Many smaller retailers now have an Internet presence, which is good for you in terms of price. Online wine buying is great for gifts; just point and click and you don't even have to wrap a gift. But when you add in the cost of shipping the prices aren't that great, unless it's a rare bottle of wine you can't find elsewhere.

Warehouse stores: If you can buy wine at warehouse stores like Costco or Sam's Club, you will save money—but you have to know what you're buying. Expensive wines will be a few dollars cheaper at these stores but they're still expensive, so don't go in thinking this is the place for bargain wine. (But the "bargain" brands, wines from huge wine companies, will still be a steal.) And remember, with the high turnover at most warehouse stores chances are you won't see the same wine on every visit.

102

Chain stores: Chain stores like California-based Beverages & More and Maryland-based Total Wines & More often have better prices because of their buying power. They should have helpful service, as well. But some small producers and specialty wines won't make it onto the shelves of these stores.

State-controlled stores: Nineteen states, including Pennsylvania and Utah, sell wine through state-controlled stores, which means that a state board has chosen what the store will sell. This means higher prices, a limited selection, and restricted hours. It doesn't look like the system will end anytime soon so you're stuck with the system unless you can get wine shipped to you or you cross state lines to buy wine. Just don't get caught; it's illegal.

Winery direct: While it's always fun to bring back a souvenir from your wine trip, remember that you're paying full retail price when you buy from a winery tasting room. But you'll often find wines that are only sold at the winery; those are the ones to stash in your suitcase. You can also get on mailing lists for small-production wines; more boutique wineries are selling their wines this way. These can be worth it for special wines that you literally won't find anywhere

else; just check out the shipping laws in your state to be sure you're not breaking them—the laws vary widely. Thirteen states prohibit direct shipments and some states even consider illegal shipping a felony. So do your homework and skip the jail time.

Wine clubs: Joining a winery wine club gives you a chance to get bottles that are available only through the winery. It's not necessarily a bargain, but worth it if (1) you love getting mail; and (2) you have the space and the desire to stash wine away. Once again, a reminder about shipping laws; check before you sign up. (A few magazines and other organizations have also started wine clubs. The wines are usually fairly priced, but you're stuck with the wines that they select.)

Auctions: Auctions are the primary selling place for old and rare wines. If you do your homework and request a catalog from an auction house in advance, you can sometimes find a few bargains for younger wines. Remember that you also have to pay a buyer's premium of 10 to 15 percent of your bid. In general, though, if you aren't investing in wine and don't have a cellar to stock, skip the auctions.

103

KOSHER
wine

Most people have eaten kosher chicken or various kosher foods, but kosher wine? Kosher wine used to be a simple, rather thick liquid made from table grapes that never went beyond the word *drinkable* (ever heard of Manischewitz?). And even though Manischewitz still accounts for 40 percent of the U.S. market, kosher wines are stepping up in quality.

The word *kosher* means that the food or drink is fit for consumption under Jewish ritual law. To be labeled "kosher" the wine has to be produced under strict guidelines, from the field to the winery, all under the supervision of a rabbi. Kosher laws require that grapes must not be used for making wine until they've reached their fourth year, no other fruits or vegetables may be grown within the vineyard, and every seventh year the fields must be left fallow. All of the tools and equipment must be kosher, and during harvest only Sabbath-observant male Jews may work on the wine and its production. During the winemaking process no animal products may be used and even the yeasts must be certified kosher. In addition, 1 percent of the wine must be discarded or given to charity as a gesture to the 10 percent tithe paid to the Levites and priests during the days of the Jerusalem Temple. (A whole other set of laws applies to wines in order to retain their kosher status once they are opened and poured by a non-Jew; these wines, called *meshuval*, are pasteurized—boiled, essentially—before bottling. There is debate about whether this changes the wine's flavor; many experts say it just changes the aging ability of the wine and not the taste.)

Kosher wines can be made from any grape varietal, and virtually every varietal is now available in kosher form. Most, but not all, wine from Israel is kosher, but virtually every winegrowing region in the world, including France, California, New Zealand, Australia, Argentina, and Chile, produces kosher wine. Even the French Champagne house Laurent-Perrier produces a kosher Champagne. A good online source for kosher wine is www.kosherwine.com.

104

Fried Zucchini Flowers

serves 4

Sometimes called squash blossoms, these delicate yellow flowers grow on zucchini vines—the female blossoms become squash and the male ones don't, but either is edible in flower form. Zucchini flowers are available in summer and early fall; farmer's markets are the best place to find them but specialty grocery stores often can get them if you ask. Because you have to eat them right away, you'll have to invite your friends into the kitchen for a glass of wine while you prepare them. I discovered these blossoms from friends in Florence, Italy, on my first-ever trip to Italy. They pair perfectly with sparkling wine, especially Italian Prosecco.

About 6 cups peanut or grapeseed oil for frying

2 large eggs

¾ cup flour

1 teaspoon salt

1 teaspoon freshly ground black pepper

2 ounces fresh mozzarella, cut into ¼-inch cubes

1 ounce prosciutto, sliced very thin and cut into 1-inch pieces

8 large zucchini flowers, gently rinsed and patted dry

1. In a large, deep sauté pan, heat 3 inches of oil to 375ºF. (Use a candy thermometer to get an accurate temperature read.)

2. In a shallow bowl, whisk the eggs. Combine the flour with the salt and pepper in another shallow bowl.

3. Wrap each cube of mozzarella with a piece of prosciutto and gently stuff it inside a zucchini flower. (The flowers tear easily, so be careful.)

4. Dip each stuffed flower first in the egg and then in the flour mixture, gently shaking off any excess flour.

5. Fry the flowers, 4 at a time, for about 2 minutes per side.

6. Drain them on a plate lined with a brown paper bag and eat immediately.

continued from page 100

Méthode Cap Classique This is South Africa's sparkling wine, made from traditional Champagne grapes in the traditional method in the coastal regions. South African sparklers are rarely more than $15; Graham Beck is one of the most respected producers.

Sekt German sparkling wine is called sekt (pronounced "ZEHKT") and is made using the Charmat method. These are fresh, fruity, slightly sweet bubblies made from Riesling and Müller-Thurgau grapes. It costs between $9 and $14.

SParKLInG wine From THE U.S.

In the United States, California in particular makes well-regarded sparkling because so many French Champagne houses set up shop there, recognizing the potential in the land and the quality grapes. Moët & Chandon were the first to arrive, establishing Domaine Chandon in Napa in 1973. Domaine Chandon was the first sparkling wine released from a French-owned California house that used the *champenoise* method. Chandon was followed by Louis Mumm, who established Napa's Mumm Cuvée; Taittinger, who created Domaine Carneros in the Napa Valley; Louis Roederer, who owns Roederer Estate in Mendocino County and also purchased its neighbor, Scharffenberger Cellars; and Piper-Sonoma in Sonoma, established by Piper-Heidsieck and now owned by J Wine Company. The Spaniards weren't far behind, with Spanish winery Freixenet establishing Gloria Ferrer in Napa's Carneros region.

California sparkling wine tends to be a bit fruitier than traditional Champagne without the yeasty flavors, but these light sparkling wines are fantastic values. There are more than thirty California wineries that produce sparkling wine, producing both vintage and nonvintage sparklers, in both *blanc de blancs* and *blanc de noirs* styles, as well as a few prestige *cuvées*. A few of the best sparkling wine producers include Domaine Chandon, Domaine Carneros, Iron Horse

Vineyards, J, Mumm, Roederer Estate, and Schramsberg Vineyards (which was the first California winery to produce a sparkling wine made by the *champenoise* method). These bubblies usually retail for $14 to $25, with some of the top cuveés running $40 to $50.

Washington, New York, and New Mexico are three other states that produce some decent bubbly. Chateau Ste. Michelle in Washington makes a well-priced apricot-colored sparkler that tastes of fresh strawberries, and Oregon's Argyle Winery produces a very nice light bubbly. The Finger Lakes region of New York makes some respectable, fragrant, fruity bubbly from the classic Champagne grape varietals as well as Riesling; they retail for around $15 to $30. Gruet Winery in New Mexico is also consistently singled out as a value sparkling wine. Started in 1983 by the Gruets, a wine family with roots in Champagne, France, the producer's seven different sparklers are made using the *champenoise* method and are Champagne-like in style—lean and intense. You can find them in most wine shops; they range from $13 to $25. While these will never be mistaken for real Champagne, they're fun to try.

continued on page 110

WINE and food PAIRING

Who needs rules? Rules are meant to be broken, as they say, but there are some guidelines to stick to so you're not left with a disappointing dinner. Trust me, poached fish does not go with Zinfandel. The fish can make the wine taste bitter and/or metallic.

Acidity: The acidity in the wine should be equal to the acidity in the dish. If not, the wine will taste dull. Because red wines lack acidity, this means sticking primarily to white wines if you're eating salad, lemon chicken, or vinegar-based dishes. (A few fresh young reds will stand up to a bit of lemon, including Beaujolais and good Lambrusco from Italy, a light fizzy red wine made from indigenous varietals; just serve them chilled.)

Bitterness: If you love bitter foods (arugula, broccoli rabe, endive), serve them with tannic wines. The bitter edge of the tannins will marry with the bitter foods. Bitter tannins will wreak havoc with fish, and some vegetables, so serve a less tannic Pinot Noir with your salmon and save the Cabernet Sauvignon and Merlot for something richer.

Salt: Tannic wines will make food seem saltier. Salt also accentuates alcohol in wine, so remember that if you're seasoning a dish you plan to serve with a big, tannic wine.

Sweets: The basic rule is that the wine has to be at least as sweet as (or sweeter than) the food. If it's not, the wine will taste tart and thin. The sweetest treats can go with heavy, sweet dessert wines like Muscats from France and Australia, sherry, and late-harvest Semillons and Rieslings. Poached fruit and fruit tarts usually pair with everything.

Spice: Spicy foods (curries, chili peppers, and so on) will make wines seem more alcoholic. For spicy food, stick to sweet wines that can counteract the spice. By sweet wines I don't mean dessert wines; I mean wines that have more fruit and may have the impression of being sweet even though there is little or no residual sugar. Whites such as Gewürztraminer, Riesling, Chenin Blanc, and Pinot Gris pair well with light, spicy dishes such as Thai food, while soft, fruity reds like Merlot and Beaujolais go well with heavier, sauce-driven spiced dishes.

Like with Like: If you are eating light food, choose lighter-style wines. The same goes for

108

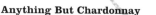

rich food; this is called the complementary approach to wine and food pairing. Balance is key to allow the wine and food magic to happen. (Although a few sweet/dessert wine combos turn that rule on its head; some desserts require lighter wines.) Another easy way to approach this principle is to think of the regionality of the wine and food; the food and wine from a region are indelibly intertwined. The rich, tangy pork and charcuterie of Alsace, France, is served with the dry, elegant Riesling, while the tomato-based and rustic meat dishes of Tuscany, Italy, are paired with lively Sangiovese. There's a reason some pairings have been around for thousands of years.

Sparkling to the Rescue: Thanks to the acidity and the bubbles (my sommelier friend Julie says the bubbles "act like little scrubbers that cleanse your palate with every sip"), dry sparkling wine goes with everything, especially foods with vinegar, lemon, capers, tomatoes, and vinaigrettes. (The one thing dry sparkling wine does not go with is sweets! Champagne and wedding cake don't mix. See facing page and page 121 for the lowdown on what to serve with dessert.)

Cheese and Wine: Cheese and wine have been served together since the invention of the cocktail party, so most people think these two are a natural pair. But it's not always wine and roses: Some cheeses are so strong that they will emphasize the tannins in the red wine and turn you off cheese and wine forever, while some white wines are overpowered by strong cheeses. The most basic (and successful) pairings include Sauvignon Blanc with goat cheese, Chardonnay with Cheddar, vintage Champagne with Parmigiano-Reggiano, Stilton with vintage Port, and Roquefort with Sauternes.

Wine and Chocolate: People love to pair wine with chocolate although few combos actually work. Fortified wines like Port generally are a seamless pairing with chocolate: Rich, velvety Port can match up to intense chocolate, as will a dark, intense Banyuls. Bubbly dessert wines like Brachetto d'Acqui from Italy can cut through the rich texture and add a zip to a chocolate dessert. Some chocolate lovers serve Cabernet Sauvignon, and while it can work, make sure you choose a fruity Cab (rather than an earthy, more herbaceous one).

109

continued from page 107

sparkling wine from australia

Although still wine is how most Americans experience Australian wine, the country produces a fair amount of sparkling (it makes up about 20 percent of total production). It's made by the *champenoise* method as well as the Charmat method from Pinot Noir and Chardonnay grapes. Champagne's Domaine Chandon has established a presence Down Under, with Domaine Chandon Australia. Australia also makes a sparkling red wine, usually from Shiraz, which is an acquired taste and rarely exported. Salinger is a top-quality sparkling producer from Australia, as is Domaine Chandon; both are made by the *champenoise* method. The wine powerhouse Foster's Yellowglen label has a line of sparklers made by the Charmat method called Pink (made from Chardonnay and Pinot Noir) and Yellow (made only from Chardonnay); these are fun budget bubbles that sell for around $9.

sparkling wine from argentina

A fair amount of sparkling wine comes from Argentina, with the French establishing a presence there like they did in California; Champagne houses such as Moët & Chandon, Mumm, and Piper-Heidsieck all have an Argentinean presence. Chandon is a great sparkling wine value, selling for around $11.

110

champagne terms

These terms are classically used for Champagne but are often used by winemakers around the world that use the *methode champenoise* to make their sparkling wine.

BEAD: The constant stream of bubbles in a glass of sparkling wine. The word refers to the bubble structure, which should run up the glass in a strandlike formation.

BLANC DE NOIRS: Indicates that the Champagne has been made using only black grapes, usually Pinot Noir and sometimes Pinot Meunier. Very rare in the Champagne region but often found among sparkling wines.

BLANC DE BLANCS: Indicates that the Champagne has been made using only Chardonnay. Not every Champagne house makes a *blanc de blancs* and they usually are more expensive than *blanc de noirs*.

CUVÉE: A blend of several varietal wines designed to become a Champagne or sparkling wine.

DOSAGE: The liqueur (sugar dissolved in reserve wine) added to the sparkling wine just before final corking. The dosage finishes the sparkling wine and determines the level of sweetness.

MOUSSE: The ring of froth or foam around the top of a glass of Champagne or sparkling wine.

NONVINTAGE: Often shortened to NV, this indicates that a Champagne was made with grapes from different years, usually three. NV Champagne contains about two thirds Pinot Noir and Pinot Meunier and one third Chardonnay and accounts for about 85 percent of all Champagne produced. This term is slowly being replaced by "multivintage," or MV, which better reflects the true method of blending several vintages' worth of grapes.

ROSÉ: A Champagne or sparkling wine whose pink tint, ranging from deep rosy pink to salmon colored, comes from the addition of a small portion of red wine to the *cuvée* before second fermentation or by letting the wine come in contact with the Pinot Noir skins. (The first method is the most

111

common and some say allows the wine to age better.) For rosé Champagne usually only Pinot Noir and Chardonnay are used. Rosé costs a bit more and not every house produces one. (It's worth repeating that this is a dry Champagne, not sweet.)

VINTAGE: Vintage Champagne is made only in years with exceptional grapes, usually about four out of every ten years. They are made with grapes from a single year and usually only from Chardonnay and Pinot Noir. It's also aged longer, usually two or more years longer than nonvintage, and has more intense, complex flavors than nonvintage Champagne. Not surprisingly, it costs considerably more.

RICOTTA PUFFS

makes about 24 puffs

These light-as-air ricotta balls prove that frying at home is worth it. Frying is easy if you remember these tips: Don't crowd the pan—allow room for the food to cook—and after each batch let the oil come back up to temperature before adding additional food. Make the batter up to two hours ahead and gather your friends in the kitchen while you fry up little balls for dessert. Serve the puffs with a sparkling dessert wine, such as Moscato d'Asti or a demi-sec (sweet) sparkling wine from Domaine Chandon or Schramsberg or demi-sec Champagne from Laurent-Perrier or Veuve Clicquot.

About 6 cups peanut or grapeseed oil for frying

1 cup all-purpose flour

1 tablespoon baking powder

Pinch of salt

4 large eggs

4 tablespoons sugar

1 pound fresh ricotta

½ teaspoon vanilla extract

Powdered sugar or honey, for serving

1. In a large, deep pot, heat the oil to 350°F. (Use a candy thermometer to get an accurate temperature read.)

2. Sift the flour, baking powder, and salt together in a small bowl.

3. Using a food processor or a whisk, mix the eggs and sugar together, then add the ricotta and the vanilla. Beat until smooth. Beat in the flour mixture until combined, but don't overmix. (The mixture will resemble thick cake batter.)

4. Drop scant tablespoonfuls of batter into the oil, about 6 at a time, and cook until golden on one side, about 1 minute. (If you use more than 1 tablespoon of batter the puffs will be too big for the center to cook all the way through.) Carefully turn them over with a slotted spoon and cook until golden on the other side.

5. Drain the puffs on a plate lined with a brown paper bag or paper towel. Dust with powdered sugar or drizzle with honey and serve immediately.

sweet wines

4

DESSERT WINES, fortified wines, DIGESTIF WINES, stickies

(as the Aussies say)—no matter how they're made, these sweet-as-honey wines can start or finish a meal (or be served any time in between).

How are they made? Two ways: Most dessert wines are made from grapes that have been left on the vine to ripen. After fermentation is stopped, a high sugar level remains (called residual sugar, or RS in wine geek-speak). The second way is by fortifying them (adding alcohol during fermentation), which stops the process and leaves residual sugar—and makes them sweet.

dessert wine basics

- Dessert wines are usually poured in two-ounce servings
- After you've uncorked it, a bottle of dessert wine will last much longer than still wine because of the sugar content.
- Pairing dessert with dessert wine can be a minefield; you

116

don't want to overpower the wine. (See page 120 for more information about pairing.) The best dessert and wine pairings occur when the dessert isn't too sweet. One caution: Chocolate and ice wine don't mix. Some dessert wines, however, aren't just for sweets. Most sweet wines are the perfect match for savory foods, such as certain cheeses and meats like foie gras and roasted duck.

"NOBLE ROT" DESSERT WINES

Noble rot, or *botrytis cinerea*, is a rot you want to get to know. This is the mold that attacks grapes and transforms them into sweet, tantalizing dessert wines. Under the right conditions botrytis causes the grapes to shrivel on the vine, concentrating the flavors and sugars, but still allows some acidity. This acidity is what keeps the wines from being overwhelmingly sweet. Noble rot can technically affect any varietal but it only happens in certain climates and usually only Sémillon, Sauvignon Blanc, Chenin Blanc, Riesling, and Gewürztraminer are used. In addition to France, Germany and Hungary produce some of the best botrytized wines, although California does make some. Far Niente in the Napa Valley makes their famous single-vineyard dessert wine "Dolce" from botrytized Sémillon and Sauvignon Blanc grapes.

Noble rot may just be the ultimate expression of "when life gives you lemons, make lemonade."

117

Sauternes

This is probably the most famous dessert wine in the world, made in the Graves district in the Bordeaux region in France from five communes, Sauternes and Barsac being the most prestigious. Pronounced "saw-TURN," it's made from three grapes (Sémillon, Sauvignon Blanc, and Muscadelle)—often called liquid gold due to their spectacularly deep yellow color (and their spectacularly high price tags). These wines are aged at least three and a half years before bottling and are then bottle-aged anywhere from five to twenty years. Sauternes are a brilliant gold color with velvety, nutty, honeyed flavors. They can be drunk young but get better when allowed to mature; ten to twenty-year-old Sauternes is exceptional, with intensified flavors and deeper color. Expect to pay at least $25 for a good Sauternes and up to several hundred dollars (especially for the most exceptional, Château d'Yquem). Sauternes is sold in regular bottles and in half bottles; some producers to look for include Château d'Arche, Château Guiraud, and Château Rieussec for Sauternes and Château Nairac and Château Climens for Barsac. Don't be fooled; "Sauterne" is made in many wine regions (sans "s") but it is not the same as the real Sauternes. Served chilled, but not ice cold, Sauternes accentuate the flavors of an apple tart, a buttery almond cake, a rich cheesecake, or poached pears. Or turn to the savory, like a piece of foie gras—or simply savor a glass on its own.

In addition to Sauternes, several dessert wines of note are made from botrytized grapes. This includes sweet wines made from Chenin Blanc grapes in the Vouvray region of the Loire Valley, including Bonnezeaux, Coteaux d'Aubance, Coteaux du Layon, Quarts de Chaume, and Vouvray Moelleux. These aren't as fat as Sauternes but show off a honeyed sweetness and deep, rich aromas; they range in price from $20 to $100. (Vouvray Moelleux is the perfect pairing with tarte tatin.) Beerenauslese (BA) and Trockenbeerenauslese (TBA) are two sweet wines made from botrytized Riesling grapes in the Mosel-Saar-Ruwer and Rheingau regions of Germany. These elegant, sweet wines are renowned as excellent values; they range from $19 to $90, a fraction of what a Sauternes commands.

118

Tokaj

This is an intense dessert wine from the Tokaj region of northern Hungary (pronounced "toe-KAI" and sometimes spelled *Tokay*) that you could almost spoon right into your mouth. Made with indigenous white grapes such as Furmint and Harslevelu as well as Muscat, these are wines with a history: They were produced well before the French made Sauternes, and the regulations for Tokaj date back to the sixteenth century. The wine is made by mashing the botrytized grapes and then adding the paste to a dry wine made with a nonbotrytized base. How much of the botrytized wine that is added determines the sweetness. The mixture ferments and is aged in caves for at least three years. The word *aszú* means "botrytis" and *puttonyos* reflects how sweet the wine is; three *puttonyos* is the least sweet and six is the sweetest. The *puttonyos* level is indicated on the label, reflecting the amount of residual sugar in the wine. Beyond six *puttonyos* is Tokaj-Aszú Essencia, with a sweetness level of about seven *puttonyos*. This is made only in the best years from the best vineyards, and is made by allowing the juice to ferment in casks for several years, without any dry wine, achieving an alcohol level of only 2 to 3 percent. (The word *puttonyos* is from the baskets used during harvest.)

After the fall of communism in 1989 Hungary dedicated itself to bringing back this wine (the vineyards had been converted to high-yield, low-quality production under communist rule); foreign investment revitalized the wine industry, and the "new" wines hit the market in 1994. Bright orange in color, they have flavors of apricots, almonds, oranges, flowers, honey, and toffee and have a higher acidity level than Sauternes, making them more refreshing on the palate. The Royal Tokaji Company is one of the most prominent producers, and other names to look for include Disznókö and Oremus. Only about 10 percent of Hungary's wine production is Tokaj, so the supply is low. It is sold in 500ml bottles and can cost anywhere from $30 to $500. Pair Tokaj with baked peaches, apricots, or any nut-based dessert.

119

PAIRING IDEAS by FOOD TYPE

ASIAN FOOD

Any Asian flavor: Bubbly

Peking duck: Pinot Gris

Dumplings: Pinot Noir, Beaujolais, rosé

Pad Thai: Riesling, Grüner-Veltliner

Sushi: Viognier, Marsanne/Roussanne, white blends

Green chicken curry: Riesling, Gewürztraminer, Torrontés

Spicy tuna tartare: sparkling wine, Riesling, Vouvray

BACKYARD BARBECUE

Pulled pork, barbequed chicken: big bold reds such as Syrah, Zinfandel, Malbec, and most red blends

Hot dogs with relish: off-dry rosé

Grilled mushrooms and vegetables: fruity red wines such as Chianti; an earthy white wine, such as Viognier and Pouilly-Fuissé

CLAMBAKE

Corn on the cob: Chardonnay, Falanghina, Marsanne

Steamed clams: Pinot Blanc, Albariño, Müller Thurgau

Lobster: Pinot Gris, Vermentino, Roussanne

SPAGHETTI AND MEATBALLS DINNER

Spaghetti and garlic bread: Any young Italian red, including Dolcetto, Barbera, Montepulciano d'Abruzzo, Sangiovese; Rioja and Pinotage would also work well

Crisp, green salad: dry Riesling, Pinot Gris, Vermentino, Muscadet

120

SOUTHERN-STYLE BRUNCH

Baked ham, biscuits, gravy: Riesling, Chenin Blanc

Fried chicken: Bubbly

Cheese grits: Chenin Blanc, Viognier, Grüner-Veltliner

Spicy gumbo: Carignan

Country-fried steak with gravy: Syrah, Shiraz, Petite Sirah

LATIN FIESTA

Peppery, garlicky red meat: Syrah, Petite Sirah

Anything with lime and cilantro: Sauvignon Blanc

Guacamole: white blend, Grüner-Veltliner, Riesling, Chablis

Spicy chicken fajitas: rosé

Beans and rice: dry rosé, Pinot Noir, Merlot

SUMMER PICNIC

Chicken salad, shrimp salad: Pinot Grigio, Pinot Gris, Chenin Blanc, Falanghina

Tomato, basil, and mozzarella panini: dry rosé

Ratatouille: dry rosé

Artichoke frittata: Chenin Blanc, Grüner-Veltliner

ITALIAN SPECIALTIES

Prosciutto and melon: Falanghina, Riesling, white Burgundy, dry Muscat

Caponata: Sauvignon Blanc, Soave

Spaghetti alla carbonara: Soave, Vermentino, Pinot Grigio

Tuscan white bean and pancetta soup: Chianti

DESSERTS

Lemon meringue pie: late-harvest Riesling

Flourless chocolate cake: late-harvest Muscat or Brachetto d'Acqui

Chocolate flan: Port, Banyuls

Cheesecake with raspberry coulis: demi-sec Champagne

Strawberry shortcake: Moscato d'Asti

Baklava: Vin Santo

CLASSIC PAIRINGS

(They don't call them classics for nothing)

Oysters: Chablis

Bouillabaisse: Provençal rosé

Stilton: vintage Port

Goat cheese: Sancerre

Roquefort: Sauternes

Foie gras: Sauternes

Boeuf bourguignon: Pinot Noir (red Burgundy)

COMFORT FOOD FAVORITES

Beef chili: Zinfandel

Grilled cheese: Chenin Blanc

Beef stew: Shiraz/Syrah, Sangiovese, Amarone

Meatloaf: Merlot

Roast chicken: Beaujolais, Chardonnay, Marsanne, Pinot Noir, Tempranillo

THE DIFFICULT FOODS

Asparagus, artichokes: Grüner-Veltliner, Sauvignon Blanc, Condrieu (Viognier), dry rosé with artichokes

Olives: Fino or Manzanilla Sherries; Rhône or Rhône-style red wine

Raw garlic: Marsanne/Roussanne, Provençal rosé

121

Late-Harvest wines

"Late harvest" means that the grapes were picked later than usual, allowing them to ripen more and develop more sugar. "Select Late Harvest" and "Special Select Late Harvest" refer to grapes picked with higher sugar levels. Australians love their "stickies," as their late-harvest wines are known, and they make two kinds of dessert wines: "noble rot" wine from Riesling and Sémillon grapes and late-harvest dessert wines from Riesling, Sémillon, Gewürtztraminer, and Sauvignon Blanc. California makes a fair amount of late-harvest wines from both methods, as do Oregon and Washington. In Alsace, France, two late harvest dessert wines are produced: Vendage Tardive, or VT, and Sélection de Grains Nobles, or SGN, are made from Riesling, Gewürtztraminer, Muscat, and Pinot Gris and only in certain years when the weather cooperates. The grapes are either left on the vine to ripen past the usual harvest date or infected with botrytis. These are what wine writer Karen MacNeil describes as "liquid ecstasy," with flavors of flowers and citrus, but are not necessarily sweet. SGN wines are always made from botrytized grapes and are sweeter than any Sauternes out there, with rich, honeyed flavors. These are rare wines that cost $45 for a half-bottle to hundreds of dollars.

Ice Wine

dinner party trivia
Canada makes more ice wine than any country in the world.

This sweet wine is made in Austria, Germany, Canada, and New York. (It gets its name from the German *Eiswein*.) The grapes freeze on the vine, and each one is handpicked and then pressed. This all happens in the middle of winter; sounds fun, no? Because the juice is frozen and the water evaporates, the sugars become extremely concentrated, resulting in a golden-colored, intensely flavored wine (the aroma is often of lychee nuts and the flavors are tropical fruit). Canada, Austria, and Germany signed an agreement and pledged to make ice wine in the official way, so any other country's "ice wine" may not be the real deal. (California producer Bonny Doon Vineyard dodges the rule by calling their version "vin de

glaciere"; it's made by artificially freezing the grapes.)

Canadian ice wine is usually made from Riesling and Vidal Blanc grapes and has about a 13 percent sugar level, which isn't very high, and the alcohol level is lower than most dessert wines, around 10 percent. You could call Canada's ice wines the poor man's Sauternes; for the price, $30 to $70, you can't beat them. You can also achieve instant gratification with ice wine: Although they'll age for up to four years, you can drink them pronto. From Canada try ice wine from Inniskillin or Mission Hill, and the Covey Run from Washington is sublime. Serve ice wine with fruit-based desserts, spicy desserts like spiced cakes, and blue-veined cheeses.

Moscato d'Asti

We should thank the Italians every day for this light, floral semisparkling dessert wine. Pronounced "mos-CAH-toe DAHS-tee," it's made with the Muscat grape in the Piemonte region; it gets its name from the village of Asti. This aromatic little wine is made by placing the grapes in tanks along with the yeast and letting them slowly ferment under cold temperatures in sealed tanks to maintain the carbon dioxide that is produced. When about half the sugar is fermented the wine is filtered and bottled. Moscato d'Asti has about 6 percent alcohol level, making it a light way to end an evening. These are not dessert wines that age; drink them within two years of the vintage date and pair them with fresh fruit or fruit tarts; skip the chocolate, though, or you'll miss all the delicate flowery components. They also make fabulous summer sippers, served as an aperitif. Some great producers to look for include Coppo, Michele Chiarlo Nivole, La Spinetta, Vietti, Bera, and Contratto. Moscato d'Asti is sold in 375ml bottles; you can find excellent Moscato d'Asti starting at $10 a bottle, and it would be hard to pay more than $20.

Another fun, fizzy dessert wine from Italy is Brachetto d'Acqui, pronounced "brah-KET-toe DAH-kwee." A semi-sweet wine made from the Brachetto grape in Piedmont, Italy, this

123

lively little wine has a deep pink color and tastes of strawberries and raspberries. The fruity, not-too-sweet flavors clamor for chocolate (especially chocolate-covered strawberries). Look for bottles from Banfi, Braida, Coppo, and Marenco; it runs $18-30.

California has also been making some wonderful late-harvest wines with various Muscat clones, including Orange Muscat, Black Muscat, and Muscat Canelli (also known as Moscato Bianco). Eberle Winery, St. Supéry, and Beaulieu Vineyard all make excellent Muscat-based dessert wines at very reasonable prices. Quady Winery makes only dessert wines; their Essencia, made from Orange Muscat grapes, is heavenly.

Recioto di Soave

This Italian dessert wine (pronounced "reh-CHAW-toh dee SWAH-veh") is from the Soave area in the Veneto region. It's made from Garganega and Trebbiano grapes using the *passito* method, similar to how Amarone is made (see page 59). The grapes are picked and then dried for about four months, concentrating the sugars, fermented, and then aged in oak barrels. The difference is that with *recioto* the fermentation is stopped before all of the sugar has converted to alcohol, so the wine is sweet. It has a yellow-gold color and tastes like dried apricots, honey, and flowers; with a 12 percent alcohol level. Recioto di Valpolicella is made in the Valpolicella region using the same method, substituting the Valpolicella grape in for the Garganega and Trebbiano. These are heady, rich wines with fruit, chocolate, and coffee elements that will hold their own against blue as well as intense soft cheeses and nut-based desserts like hazelnut cake and pine nut cookies as well as the classic Italian fruitcake panettone. Sold in 375ml and 500ml bottles, it runs $17 to $80.

124

Vin Santo

Last but certainly not least is Vin Santo (pronounced "veen SAHN-toh"), a sweet Italian wine made from Malvasia and/or Trebbiano grapes, although the types of grapes vary according to the region. Most Vin Santo comes from Tuscany, but Alto Adige, Umbria, and the Veneto produce some too. A lot of love goes into this wine, which is made by a very labor- and time-intensive process.

The grapes are picked late in the season and then hung in an airy room to dry for three to six months; and as the grapes dry and the water evaporates, the sugars get concentrated. Although every family and wine estate uses a slightly different method, the grapes are crushed, and the grape juice, or must, ferments and then ages for three to six years in oak or chestnut barrels called *caratelli* in warm attics called *vinsantaia*. But this isn't an ordinary "sweet" wine; this deep-orange-colored wine has deep honey, caramel, and nut flavors, and a few are made into dry styles; the alcohol level ranges from 14 to 17 percent.

These wines were originally only produced and consumed by families, only later becoming available commercially (around the fourteenth century). Vin Santo is considered a wine of hospitality in Italy, almost always served to guests with a plate of crisp biscotti for dipping, but they're excellent with any nut-based dessert.

Look for Vin Santo from Avignonesi, Badia, Castellare, Felsina, Selvapiana, and Isole e Olena. Vin Santo is sold in 375ml or 500ml bottles and runs $20 to well over $100. (But don't worry too much about opening an expensive bottle; an open bottle of Vin Santo will keep for up to a year.)

Sherry

This famous Spanish wine deserves a whole chapter to explain its nuances, but here are the basics. A fortified wine, sherry is made by adding grape spirits to the wine after fermentation (Palomino is the grape varietal used). It is produced only in the Andalucia region of Spain in two basic styles, fino (dry, crisp, almond

continued on page 130

dinner party trivia
The word *sherry* comes from the British mispronunciation of Jerez (pronounced "HEH-reth" in Spain), a town where many bodegas are located.

125

WHAT to POUR and HOW to PLAN

Throwing a wine-tasting party may sound involved, but nothing could be simpler. Whether you're inviting novices, dabblers, or experienced wine lovers, arranging a tasting is a great way to entertain—and learn something in the process.

First things first: Decide what kind of tasting you want to do. Generally, choosing one varietal and serving several examples from various regions is the best way to compare the different styles. For example, you can explore the regional differences of Sauvignon Blanc by opening bottles from California, France, New Zealand, South Africa, and South America. But the possibilities are endless: Pick a country and explore its major wines, or pick one region and try several different producers (compare Napa Valley Cabernet Sauvignons, Pinot Noirs from Sonoma County, or different Champagnes from Champagne, France). Invent your own themes, such as Think Pink (a Rosé tasting), Sweet Stuff (dessert wines), Get Screwed (screw-cap wines), or Port of Call (an assortment of Ports). You can also decide on price point—try tasting Rieslings under $20 or $30 Syrah. Including a broad range of price points is an effective way to see just how much price plays into the quality of the wine.

Talking to a wine retailer can inspire ideas, and often a retailer will be excited to help you find different bottles that may surprise your guests. Six to eight wines is usually a good number to start with for a tasting; more than eight and guests tend to get overwhelmed.

Most professional tastings are conducted blind; this ensures total neutrality and objectiveness on the part of the tasters. In a casual setting, blind tastings not only add to the fun but often the unveiling of the wines is the best part of the night. The easiest way to hide the label is to stick each wine bottle in a brown paper lunch bag and then number the bags starting with the number one. Create a master list of the wines that includes the producer name, retail price, and corresponding bag number, and keep it hidden from the guests until the end of the tasting. (Wine tasting parties are a fine time to go BYOB. Not only does it lessen the stress on the host, the variety in the wines presented is wider. If you're having guests bring bottles, just add them to the list as guests arrive.) After everyone has tasted the wines, unveil the bags—this usually prompts even more discussion.

After you've decided on the varietal(s), set the head count. This will determine the number of wine glasses you need. Ideally you should use the same type of wine glass for each person, but if push comes to shove any wine glasses will do. (See page 42 for more on wine glasses.) If you're serving red and white wine it's nice to have two different glasses, but it's not crucial. For

126

Port, Sherry, and some dessert wines, it's nice to have glasses that show off their characteristics, but again, it's not mandatory.

A standard tasting pour is two ounces. (Guests can always go back at the end and pour themselves a glass of their favorite.) Start with the white wines (including bubbly), move to red wines, and end with sweet wines. Within that framework, start with lighter-bodied wines and end with the heavier wines. One tip: In between the wines, rinse the glasses with the new wine, not with water. (Although guests will appreciate glasses of water.) Place empty pitchers or buckets on the table to be used as both spit buckets and as dump buckets for any leftover wine. Be sure to have baskets of neutral-flavored crackers or sliced bread for people to nibble on during the tasting. To fully enjoy the wine, it's best to serve appetizers or dinner items after the tasting so the flavors don't influence the perception of the wine, but it's up to you to decide how professional you want a tasting to be.

Tasting sheets are a great way for people to write down their thoughts about each wine. Many different wine-tasting sheets are available to download online from wine magazines and wine enthusiast sites and include a space for the appearance, aroma or nose, taste, finish, and overall quality of the wine. If you have a truly geeky crowd, you can use tasting sheets that have points. The standard is 100 points, although 20-point sheets are easier for the novice to use. But you can also throw the number/scoring system to the wind and just have guests write down their thoughts; the ultimate question is if they would buy a particular wine again. If you're going for an informal, chatty type of tasting, tasting sheets aren't necessary. But at the very least you should have a list of every wine served for people to take home with them in case they want to buy a bottle. And don't forget pens!

Last but not least, have fun. Many people are intimidated about what to say or what to think about wine, and your job as host is to get them to relax and enjoy the process. After all, it's just wine.

127

STRAWBERRY-RHUBARB TART

serves 6 to 8

This is a take on the French galette, a rustic, free-form tart, perfect for those with a fear of pastry. The dough is very simple to make, but you can substitute a store-bought pie shell, thawed and rolled out to ⅛-inch thickness. A spoonful of tangy crème fraîche brings the dessert together and makes it a match for a Moscato d'Asti or a glass of late-harvest dessert wine.

For the tart dough

1 cup all-purpose flour

½ teaspoon sugar

Pinch of salt

6 tablespoons cold unsalted butter, cut into ½-inch pieces

¼ cup very cold water

For the filling

3 tablespoons fine plain breadcrumbs

5 tablespoons plus 1 teaspoon sugar (see Notes)

½ teaspoon cinnamon

1 heaping cup strawberries, hulled and quartered (see Notes)

2 cups chopped rhubarb (½-inch pieces, from 6 stalks, about ¾ pound; see Notes)

2½ tablespoons all-purpose flour

1 teaspoon freshly squeezed lemon juice

½ teaspoon vanilla extract

2 tablespoons heavy cream or milk

Crème fraîche, for serving

1. Preheat the oven to 400°F.

2. Make the tart dough: In the bowl of a food processor, pulse together the flour, sugar, and salt. Add the butter and pulse until the mixture resembles coarse meal. Sprinkle the water over the mixture and pulse just until a dough forms. (Any longer than that and the dough will be tough.) Shape the dough into a flat disk, wrap with plastic wrap, and refrigerate for at least 30 minutes. (You can make the dough up to 2 days ahead; just keep it tightly wrapped in plastic wrap in the refrigerator.)

3. In a small bowl combine the breadcrumbs with the 1 teaspoon sugar and ¼ teaspoon of the cinnamon. Set aside.

4. In another bowl combine the strawberries, rhubarb, the remaining 5 tablespoons sugar, flour, lemon juice, vanilla, and remaining ¼ teaspoon cinnamon.

5. On a lightly floured surface, roll out the dough (or a store-bought pie shell) to ⅛-inch thickness, about a 14-inch round. Transfer the dough to a baking sheet. (If the dough tears, just pinch it back together.)

128

6. Sprinkle the breadcrumb mixture over the dough round, leaving a 2-inch border around the edge. Cover the breadcrumbs with the fruit mixture. Carefully lift the edges of the dough up and partly over the fruit, folding and overlapping the dough. (There will be about a 4-inch opening in the middle, exposing the fruit.) Using a pastry brush, brush the edges of the dough with the milk or cream.

7. Bake for 45 to 50 minutes, until golden brown. (If the fruit in the middle starts to brown before the crust, cover it with a small piece of aluminum foil.) Let cool for at least 10 minutes before serving. Serve with a bowl of crème fraîche.

notes: Depending on how sweet the strawberries are, you may need to add up to 2 additional tablespoons sugar.

Frozen strawberries won't work in this recipe; they will just dissolve into jam when baked. Dried strawberries, however, are a perfect substitute in winter; use 3 tablespoons dried chopped strawberries.

Frozen rhubarb works well; just thaw it slightly. When using fresh rhubarb, trim every bit of the leaves; they are toxic.

continued from page 125

aromas) and oloroso (dry, dark, nutty, rich, walnut aromas). Sweet sherries are made by sweetening either of the two types.

The difference between fino and oloroso is their exposure to oxygen: fino sherry develops a *flor*, a type of yeast, which covers the wine and prevents oxygen from getting in, while oloroso is exposed to oxygen to give it a nutty flavor and dark color. The sherry is then aged in casks in dry *bodegas* (the Spanish word for a wine cellar or wine-producing company), which allows some of the water to evaporate. The aging process happens in a way that is unlike any other method of winemaking: The wine is added to the casks of older wines, and some of the older wine is added to casks of even older wine; this can go on for many generations, and it's a process called the *solera* system. This is why there is no vintage date on most sherry.

The fino and oloroso sherries then become many types of sherry, based on their age. These include Manzanilla, Amontillado, and Palo Cortado. Sweet sherry is made by adding a sweetener, usually the juice of dried grapes. Types of sweet sherry include Cream Sherry, Brown Sherry, and Pedro Ximénez. (A few producers make sherry outside the official sherry DO region of Jerez, and these are usually less expensive. A decent bottle will cost between $10 and $15.)

Some reliable sherry producers include Osborne, Emilio Lustau, and Sandeman. Dry sherries can be served with a variety of savory snacks, from roasted nuts and olives to cheese, sausage, and cured meats. Sweet sherries are often served as digestifs but will work with desserts such as cheesecake, fruit tarts, and any chocolate confection.

Port

If you thought making Champagne was complicated, imagine the task faced by the winemakers who work with the more than 80 varietals that can be used to make Port. Port is a fortified wine (about four parts wine to one part brandy). The addition of brandy kills the yeast, stopping the fermentation process and resulting in a sweet, high-alcohol wine (about 20 percent).

It's made in Portugal with grapes from the Douro Valley, five red grapes being the most important. Other wine-producing countries make their own versions of "port," but they're not the same thing; real Porto only comes from Portugal.

There are two major distinctions for Port: Ruby and Tawny. Ruby Port is aged in bottles, while Tawny is aged in casks. There are seemingly endless types of Port, but these are the major ones that will get you started.

• **Ruby Port:** This is young Port with bright fruit and little bottle-age and is the most affordable, usually about $10 a bottle. "Fine" or "Reserve" indicates higher quality.

• **Tawny Port:** These are more complex examples, aged in wood and with more spice and nut flavors. The best tawnies show their age on the label (ten, twenty, thirty years, and older). Tawnies cost anywhere from $15 up to $60 for the oldest Ports.

• **Vintage Character Port:** This is Ruby Port blended with grapes from several vintages and aged before bottling. These are full-bodied Ports that are ready to drink at about $16 a bottle. Don't look for "Vintage Character Port" on the label; it's not always there. Each house has a special brand name for its vintage character Port: for example, Fonseca "Bin 27," Graham's "Six Grapes," and Cockburn's "Special Reserve."

• **Late Bottled Vintage Port (LBV):** This is Port made from grapes from a declared vintage, aged and ready to drink. You can find LBV for around $20 a bottle.

• **Vintage Port:** This is the crème de la crème of Port. It is made from grapes grown in a single year from the best vineyards. But before you get excited, you have to realize that vintage Port usually needs to age at least twenty years from the vintage date. So patience, my friend. That will give you time to pay off the $50 you spent on a bottle. (Vintage port only makes up only about 2 percent of all the Port produced.)

With Port, you can't go wrong with these legendary names: Graham, Fonseca, Dow, Taylor (also known as Taylor-Fladgate), and Sandeman.

Break out a bottle of Port to serve with a strong cheese like Roquefort, Stilton, or aged Cheddar or nut-based desserts like hazelnut torte.

THE OTHER
wine REGIONS

While France, California, and Australia are among the most familiar wine regions in the world, grapes are grown—and wine is made—in countries spanning the globe. Countries as far-flung as Indonesia, Korea, and India are making wine; here are a few lesser-known countries worth exploring in your ABC quest.

Greece

It was only a few years ago that most Americans equated Greek wine with low-quality blends and pine-scented retsina, but winemakers have changed course in the past ten years, using modern techniques to produce high-quality wines that are changing the face of the Greek wine industry.

Wine is certainly nothing new to Greece, where the first vines were planted four thousand years ago. With three hundred days of sun, low average rainfall, varied soils, and the proximity to the sea, viticulture flourishes. The five hundred wineries in this mountainous country produce wine from ten regions, ranging from the snowy mountains of Macedonia in the north to the sun-drenched islands of the southern Aegean.

White wines were traditionally the backbone of the Greek wine industry, making up 40 percent of production, but in the past ten years the reds have caught up. International varietals, including Cabernet Sauvignon, Syrah, Merlot, Chardonnay, and Sauvignon Blanc are being planted alongside the more than three hundred indigenous varietals, including Agiorgitiko, Xinomavro, and Mavrodaphne. Both indigenous and international varietals are being made into fresh and lively rosés, while late-harvest and fortified wines made from Muscat and Mavrodaphne varietals are some of the best-value sweet wines in the world.

The most well known Greek producers include Boutari, Domaine Gerovassiliou, Evharis, Gaia Estate, Sigalas, and Tsantali. Other notable estates in Macedonia include Biblia Chora, started by Evangelos Gerovassiliou and Vassilis Tsaktsarlis, focusing on organic wines, Katogi Strofilia, and Alpha Estate. These are extremely food-friendly wines that are distributed nationally, although most appear in restaurants; they retail from $9 to $50.

132

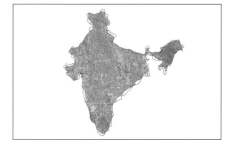

India

Although India has been growing grapes since the seventeenth century, viticulture in a tropical latitude is challenging. The grapes never go dormant, which means a lot of time in the vineyard, not to mention the problem of storing wine in the sweltering Indian heat. But since the early 1980s India has been trying its hand at making high-quality wine, planting red and white varietals and making both still and sparkling wines. Cabernet Sauvignon, Shiraz, Clairette, Chardonnay, Viognier, and Sauvignon Blanc are planted in southern and western India. India has generally been a spirits-driven market, but with a growing young population that is drinking more wine than ever before, more wineries are setting up shop. Winemakers from France and California have been advising some Indian wineries; Sula Winery hired Sonoma County winemaker Kerry Damsky as a consultant, and Grover Vineyards built its winery with the former winemaker of the French Champagne house Mumm (and hired renowned French wine consultant Michel Rolland to help make the wine). Chateau Chougule and Chateau Indage (known for making the first sparkling wine in India) are two other producers making wine worth trying; it usually costs around $10 a bottle.

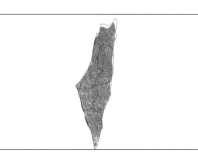

Israel

In the late nineteenth century French winemaker Baron Edmond de Rothschild invested a significant amount in Israel's wine industry which led to the planting of both red and white French varietals such as Carignan, Cabernet Sauvignon, Merlot, Grenache, Chenin Blanc, Muscat, Riesling, and Chardonnay. Despite the heat, many vineyards flourish in the five wine regions (Galilee, or Galil, and Golan Heights are considered the best), and with many California-trained winemakers the wine industry started producing internationally recognized wines in the early 1980s. Some of the wines are kosher but many boutique wineries produce nonkosher wine. A smattering of boutique wineries have opened in Israel in the past ten years, but the best producers are Barkan and Segal's as well as Yaden and Gamla, two labels from Golan Heights Winery. Israeli wines usually cost between $9 and $20 a bottle.

Lebanon

Although ancient civilizations made a lot of wine in Lebanon, decades of war and other historical events have prevented a major winemaking industry from flourishing. Not surprisingly, French influence is strong. Although some Chardonnay is produced and there are some white grape plantings, the focus is on reds from Cabernet Sauvignon, Merlot, Mourvedre, Syrah, Grenache, Cinsault, and Carignan. There is one wine region called the Bekaa Valley. Chateau Comte de M. Kefraya is one of Lebanon's oldest wineries and Chateau Ksara is one of the largest. A must-try is the Musar blend from the legendary Chateau Musar, established in 1930. This blend of Cabernet Sauvignon, Cinsault, and Carignan is aged seven years before it's released and can age up to fifteen years. With deep fruit, chocolatey flavors, and hints of cedar it is stunning with lamb. Lebanese wines run $13 for the most basic up to hundreds of dollars for Chateau Musar.

Mexico

While you may think tequila is Mexico's only beverage, there are plenty of wines coming from the Baja region near the Pacific Ocean. Wine arrived in Mexico along with the Spanish priests during the colonial era and the Baja climate has been touted as similar to that of California's Napa Valley. But trade barriers, water shortages, and high domestic taxes (40 percent per bottle) have prevented a true wine renaissance. Mexican winemakers seem to be planting everything: Reds such as Petite Sirah, Cabernet Sauvignon, Nebbiolo, Merlot, Grenache, and Zinfandel and white varietals such as Chardonnay, Sauvignon Blanc, and Chenin Blanc are going into surprisingly delicious wines. Producers such as Cavas Valmar, Casa Madero, Casa de Piedra, Monte Xanic, Santo Tomas, and Vinos L.A. Cetto are worth trying. The export market is limited, with much of it going to restaurants, but in the United States most Mexican wines retail for around $10 to $20.

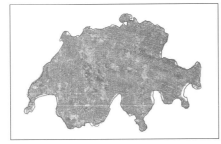

Switzerland

Although chocolate and watches are Switzerland's more famous exports, there are over twenty thousand winegrowers in this mountainous country and a history of wine that dates back to Roman times. Since the end of World War II Swiss winemaking has become modernized and focused on higher-quality wines. There are five regions, Vanais being the largest. White indigenous varietals historically dominated, but grapes such as Merlot, Gamay, Cabernet Sauvignon, and Pinot Noir now account for much of the red wine production. The most exported Swiss wines are white wines, including Fendant (the Swiss name for the grape Chasseras), Sylvaner, and Müller Thurgau. In the past few years Merlot from the region of Ticino has attracted some attention. But the Swiss keep most of the wine for themselves, exporting around 1 percent of the total production. Reliable producers include Robert Gilliard; most retail for around $22 to $29.

Uruguay

Tucked between Brazil and Argentina is Uruguay, the land of Tannat. Tannat (pronounced "tah-NAHT") is a harsh, tannic varietal originally from France that becomes softer and riper in Uruguay. Reds dominate here, and besides Tannat, which makes up about a third of the total production, varietals such as Merlot, Syrah, and Petite Sirah and a few whites are the most common varietals. There are nine wine regions, the best of which is Salto, but the regions are less important than the producers when choosing wines from Uruguay. Uruguay's wine industry is made up of three hundred wineries with few exports, but if you can find them these big, spicy, intense reds are worth trying—if only to say that you did. Open a bottle alongside a piece of beef and see what the fuss is about. Good producers include Ariano, Bouza, Torrens, Viñedo de los Vientos, Monte de Luz, Stagnari, and Pisano. Prices of Tannat run the gamut; you'll see bottles under $10 and up to $30.

Madeira

Another fortified wine from Portugal, this time from the island of Madeira, these wines are fortified and then slowly cooked after fermentation in casks using the estufagem process or, for the finest Madeira, heated naturally using sunlight. (The word *maderized* means the wine is oxidized through heating.) Because they're oxidized and fortified, containing 17 to 20 percent alcohol by volume, a bottle of Madeira can literally last forever in your kitchen cupboard, just like any other spirit.

Madeira was a happy accident; in the 1600's shipping wine was a treacherous business, with spoilage being a major roadblock, so producers started adding a bit of neutral spirits to keep the wine fresh. After a long, hot journey producers realized the heated, fortified wine was even better than before, and Madeira was born. Although Madeira was considered *the* beverage in the American colonies in the eighteenth century, Madeira has lost a bit of its prestige since then. The quality has been unpredictable, ranging from cheap swill to an extremely complex wine, and these days more Americans cook with Madeira than drink it.

Pronounced "muh-DARE-uh," it's made from one of four white grapes (Bual, Malmsey, also known as Malvasia, Sercial, and Verdelho) as well as the red grape Tinta Negra Mole. (Interestingly, Madeira is technically a white wine.) There are four sweetness levels that correspond to the white varietal names; from driest to sweetest they are Sercial, Verdelho, Bual, and Malmsey. Additionally, there are four basic styles depending on aging: three year old (made from Tinta Negra Mole grapes, no wood aging); five year old (some wood aging); ten year old (aged in cask); and frasqueira (vintage Madeira, highest quality; aged 20 years in cask after the heating process and made only from the white varietals). Both vintage and non-vintage Madeira is produced. The most basic, low-end Madeira is bulk, made from Tinta Negra Mole grapes, and it gets its color from caramel coloring. In the United States Madeira is often found more in the kitchen than on a wine rack. When used in cooking Madeira adds a richness to dishes, particularly soups, sauces, and sautéed mushrooms; just be sure to skip the

136

bottles labeled "madeira" (lower case "m;" these are cheap jug wines and are not the real deal).

This intense, amber-colored wine has flavors of baked fruit, toffee, and caramel with a nice level of acidity. Madeira is one wine that work spectacularly with chocolate but it's not restricted to sweets; it makes an unlikely yet tasty aperitif. The sweetest Madeira styles can also be served as a dessert themselves. Serve the drier styles at a cool temperature and the sweeter ones at room temperature. Madeira will set you back anywhere from $14 to $40 and is sold in both 500mL and 750mL bottles (expect to pay more for vintage Madeira); look for bottles from Blandy's, Broadbent, Cossart Gordon, and Leacock's.

Vins Doux Naturels (VDN)

Sweet, fortified wines have been made in the Languedoc-Roussillon region of France since the thirteenth century (Vins doux Naturels, normally referred to as VDN, means "naturally sweet wine" in French). Most are made from the Muscat grape but a Grenache-based version called Banyuls, pronounced "bahn-YOOLZ," is one to grab. Banyuls is a rich, dark, Port-like dessert wine with flavors of coffee, mocha, and dark plum that pairs magnificently with chocolate, from an elegant chocolate torte or an airy chocolate souffle to the most basic chocolate cupcakes. (The latest culinary craze is Banyuls vinegar, a rich, dark vinegar aged in oak casks that is available in specialty food stores.) By law Banyuls must contain 15 percent alcohol and be made from at least 50 percent Grenache. Banyuls Grand Cru must be aged a minimum of 30 months and made from at least 75 percent Grenache. As with Muscat de Beaumes-de-Venise, these wines are made by stopping the fermentation of the grapes by adding a neutral, clear brandy part-way through the fermentation process.

continued on page 141

137

NINE WINES you've NEVER HEARD OF
(but will love)

While ten years ago you probably wouldn't have found any of these wines in your local wine shop or on a restaurant wine list, more native varietals are making their way to the American wine market. And aren't we lucky—these are lesser-known wines that can be great bargains, and they're all supremely food-friendly, to boot. Most of these names won't roll off the tip of your tongue, but once you taste them you'll be hooked.

. . . .

Aglianico

This dry, robust red wine is made from the Aglianico (pronounced "ah-LYAH-nee-koh") grape in southern Italy. Don't be put off by the pronunciation; you don't need to be able to say it well to enjoy a glass. (Along with Nebbiolo and Sangiovese, Aglianico is considered one of Italy's three noble grape varietals.) The regions of Campania and Basilicata produces reds that are meant for aging, needing time—usually six to nine years—to tame the tannins and acidity and bring out the chocolaty, earthy, and dark fruit flavors; some can even age 15 years or longer. Try this intense red with hearty dishes such as spaghetti with meat ragù, roast beef, grilled lamb chops, pizza, or any hard aged cheese. The most prestigious regions for Aglianico are Campania's Taurasi DOCG and Basilicata's Aglianico del Vulture DOC, which will

be indicated on the label. These rich reds cost a bit more, usually $20 to $55 retail, although less impressive bottles go for $8 to $15. Aglianico from producers such as Alovini, Bisceglia, Contado, Donato D'Angelo, and Terra de Re is your best bet.

Arneis

Arneis is another gem from Italy's Piedmont region. (The specific area where it's grown is called Roero, a DOC, and is indicated on the label.) Often called Piedmont's answer to Pinot Grigio, this feisty white made a comeback in the 1980s and medium-bodied, aromatic wines that taste of apricots, apples, and pears are the result. Pronounced "ahr-NAZE," this is a fabulous seafood wine that also pairs with chicken, pork, pasta dishes, and even bolder flavors like smoked trout. Drink Arneis within two years of the vintage date. (A few

138

California producers have planted Arneis but the general consensus is to stick with the Italian stuff.) Some producers to look for include Castello di Neive, Ceretto, Giacosa, Matteo Correggia, and Vietti; it retails for around $12 to $30.

Orvieto

This just might be the ultimate picnic wine. Named after the town in the region of Umbria, Italy, where it's produced, this crisp white wine (pronounced "ohr-vee-YET-oh") is made primarily from the Trebbiano grape along with several native varietals such as Grechetto, Malvasia, and Verdello. There are two classifications for Orvieto: Orvieto and Orvieto Classico, the classico being the superior wine. If you like simple, fresh white wine, Orvieto is your new best friend. This isn't one for cellaring, so buy it and drink it pronto. Because of its bold acidity, Orvieto pairs perfectly with a variety of dishes, from simple sandwiches and potato or shrimp salad to more complex, coconut milk-based dishes. Look for Orvieto Classico from Antinori, Barberani, Bigi, Conte Vaselli, Palazzone, Salviano, and Ruffino. Orvieto retails for under $10, with better bottles selling for around $15.

Malvasia Bianca

This is a fun, feisty wine if there ever was one. Pronounced "mahl-va-ZEE-ah bee-AHN-ka," this aromatic Italian white varietal will tickle your palate with spice, citrus, and tropical fruit flavors. (The name is often shortened to simply Malvasia; the "Bianca" is used to distinguish it from its red cousin, Malvasia Nera.) This is a light-bodied wine with low tannins, and it runs the gamut from dry to sweet, and low to high alcohol. On the islands of Sardinia and Sicily it's often made into a sparkling wine and fortified and made into rare *passito* dessert wines. It's grown widely throughout Italy, and the Italians blend it with the white varietal Trebbiano. The best dry Malvasia in Italy comes from Friuli, and are very floral and fruity. It also ends up in red wines, particularly in the region of Lazio, and is made into Vin Santo in Tuscany. In Spain it's blended with Macabeo and it provides the base for Madeira (see page 136). California has had particular success with this varietal, making off-dry table wines as well as dessert wines with 100 percent Malvasia Bianca grapes. Other than dessert wines you should drink these up pronto. Try dry Malvasia with light seafood dishes and the heavier styles with grilled fish; it also pairs with the flavors of Thai, Chinese, and Vietnamese cuisines. (See page 120 for more on pairings.) Italian examples can be hard to find; you'll most likely encounter them on restaurant wine lists that specialize in Italian wines. California producers such as Bonny Doon (the Ca' del Solo label), Drytown Cellars, Palmina, and Wild Horse are making single varietal examples worth sipping; they retail for $10 to $20.

Gavi

This crisp, dry white wine is named for a town in Piedmont, Italy. Made from a native Piemontese grape called Cortese (that some say is the region's best white wine), Gavi gained a more prestigious DOCG wine classification in 1998. The wine estate La Scolca is credited with bringing this wine, pronounced "GAH-vee," to the forefront of the wine world in the 1960s. Many top examples come from the seaside area of Liguria, which explains the wine's affinity for seafood. The wines retail from around $14 to $40 for the top of line examples; drink them young, within two years of the vintage date. (Some Gavi is labeled as Cortese, so don't be confused.) Look for

Gavi from La Scolca (called Gavi di Gavi), as well as Dezzani, Fontanafredda, Pio Cesare, Michele Chiarlo, and Villa Sparina.

Nero d'Avola

For a rich red with soft tannins, look no further than this indigenous varietal from Sicily. Pronounced "neh-roe DAH-vo-lah," this feisty red is great to drink now but gets even better with age, emphasizing the big fruit and earthy flavors. (It's often compared to Syrah.) While Nero d'Avola was once relegated to a blending grape or a sad red table wine, Sicilian winemakers are now making better-quality examples and it is certainly one of the best-value food wines around. Think of bold, wild, spicy flavors when it comes to food pairings: serve it with fiery pasta puttanesca, broccoli rabe, anchovy and black olive pizza, or just a simple grilled steak. Nero d'Avola retails for $10 to $35 a bottle, depending on the producer, but you can get a decent bottle for around $12. Mirabile, Morgante (and their higher priced line, Morgante Don Antonio), Planeta, Regaleali, Santa Anastasia, Spadina, and Valle dell'Acate are producers to look for.

Torrontés

This white varietal is Argentina's signature white grape, pronounced "tor-RON-tez." It makes a lively aromatic wine, with melon, green apple, orange blossom, and tropical fruit flavors. (Some call it Argentina's answer to Viognier, and DNA research has shown that it's related to Malvasia.) What makes it even better is that you can find a fabulous bottle for under $15 (it retails between $6 to $15). Drink it chilled while you're lying on the sofa, or pair it with dinner: A cheese plate, smoked meat, pork, or fish (especially shellfish) will complement the fresh flavors. Bodega Colome, Crios de Susana Balbo,

Crisol, and Plata make lip-smacking examples.

Verdicchio

Yet another native white varietal of Italy, this crisp yet elegant wine is perfect for sipping or with a meal. Made in the Marches region and pronounced "vehr-DEEK-kyoh," it is a medium-bodied wine that has an almost nutty characteristic with hints of peaches and apples. It's made with the addition of Trebbiano and Malvasia grapes, the two grapes legally permissible in the blend under Italian wine laws. The best Verdicchio comes from the DOC of Verdicchio dei Castelli di Jesi, which will be written on the label. A fabulous food wine, try Verdicchio with light dishes such as raw seafood, braised or fresh fennel, pasta tossed with olive oil and garlic, or even veal saltimbocca. A bottle of Verdicchio will set you back between $8 and $40, depending on the producer. Some great producers include Bucci, Fazi Battaglia, Laila, and Sartarelli.

Vernaccia

What is it with Italy and indigenous grape varietals? This tasty white from Italy, Vernaccia, pronounced "vehr-NAHT-chah," is medium-bodied and full of honey, flowers, pear, citrus, and mineral notes—and no oak. Grown in Tuscany, and officially known as Vernaccia di Gimignagno (for the hill town where it's grown), Vernaccia is considered Tuscany's best white wine (it has its own DOCG). This little grape sings with a variety of dishes, from white bean dip and steamed mussels to seared tuna and spicy Thai food—and even guacamole. Drink it young, within two years of the vintage date, although some *riservas* are said to age for three to five years. Look for bottles by Cesani, Contini, Falchini, and Teruzzi & Puthod; Vernaccia retails for around $14 a bottle.

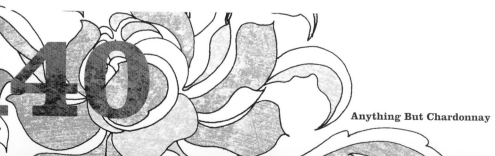

continued from page 137

VDN's are 16 to 17 percent alcohol and are sold in 375mL or 500mL bottles; most cost $25 to $60. These wines can be hard to find but producer M. Chapoutier makes a wonderful Banyuls that is available in the States.

Beaumes-de-Venise

Muscat de Beaumes-de-Venise, pronounced "bohm-duh-vuh-NEEZ," is one of the best known VDN's, made from the Muscat grape. A sweet wine from the Rhône region of France, it's produced by halting the fermentation of the grapes by adding a neutral brandy, resulting in a sweet, rich wine with good acidity (this method is called *mutage*). These wines have aromas of roses and taste like peaches, apricots, apples, and grapes but they're not as viscous as most dessert wines. Serve it with fresh fruit peaches and figs, desserts such as banana cream tarts and sticky toffee pudding, or intense blue cheeses like Gorgonzola and Roquefort but don't just save it for dessert; in France Muscat de Beaumes-de-Venise is often served as an aperitif.

Great producers include Paul Jaboulet Aîné, Domaine de Durban, and Vidal Fleury. Sold in 375mL bottles, they cost between $15 and $45.

141

SPICED CHOCOLATE MOUSSE

serves 6

This intense chocolate mousse has a kick, accented with spices and ending with a crunch. It pairs perfectly with both Port and Port-style dessert wines, Muscat-based dessert wines, as well as Brachetto d'Acqui.

7 ounces high-quality bittersweet chocolate

4 large eggs, separated (see Note)

4 teaspoons sugar

¼ cup strong brewed espresso, at room temperature

Pinch of ground cloves

¼ teaspoon ground cayenne pepper

½ teaspoon cinnamon

⅛ teaspoon freshly grated nutmeg

⅔ cup cold heavy cream

6 teaspoons cocoa nibs, for garnish (available in most gourmet stores in the baking section)

1. Put water in the bottom of a double boiler and bring it to a simmer. (Alternatively, use a saucepan filled halfway with water and place a mixing bowl on top.) Add the chocolate to the top of the double boiler and stir until melted. Remove from the heat and let cool slightly.

2. Place the egg yolks in a bowl and mix in the sugar, beating until pale and creamy. Add the cooled melted chocolate and the espresso and whisk until thoroughly combined. Add the cayenne pepper, cinnamon, and nutmeg and whisk until thoroughly combined.

3. Using a hand mixer or whisk, whip the cream until it is stiff. Fold it into the chocolate mixture until no white appears.

4. In another bowl, whip the egg whites until stiff peaks form. Using a spatula, gently fold them into the chocolate mixture, being careful so as to not to deflate them; there may be a few streaks of white but the majority should be fully incorporated.

5. Spoon the mousse into individual serving bowls or into one large serving bowl, cover with plastic wrap, and refrigerate for at least 4 hours or overnight.

5. Before serving, sprinkle the top of each bowl with 1 teaspoon of cocoa nibs.

note: Raw eggs carry a small risk of salmonella. If that's a concern to you, use pasteurized eggs, available in most grocery stores.

142